Over the years Dr. John Whitcomb has shared his "Capitation Method" for raising financially responsible teens with parents. Here's what they, and others, are saying about

Dr. John Whitcomb's guide for raising financially astute and mature children is more than a how-to. It is a philosophy of learning financial responsibility.

—*Elizabeth Meyer, Former Reporter/Researcher for* Time *Magazine*

This is a book that will bring a smile to the hearts and wallets of parents! Dr. Whitcomb lends humor and a great deal of insight to the serious subject of teaching kids about money. Parents will chuckle as they see themselves and their kids on these pages! But the real profit lies in the wealth of ideas Dr. Whitcomb gives on teaching money management to kids.

—*Sharon Koenings, Director of College Admissions and College Counseling and Assistant Head, Brookfield Academy, Brookfield, Wisconsin*

Capitate Your Kids provides an effective solution to teaching kids not only the value of money but other values they will use throughout their lifetime.

—*Carl Schultz, CPA and Partner, Suby Von Haden, Milwaukee, Wisconsin*

Before reading *Capitate Your Kids,* I had been frustrated with having to deal with my kids coming to me for money on a daily and weekly basis. Once I got them on a budget, they learned they had choices about working, school, and extracurricular opportunities, and that those choices lead to sacrifices and consequences. I was never happier, because I no longer had to make those difficult choices for them.

—*Mike Hargarten, Financial Representative, Northwestern Mutual Financial Network*

Capitate Your Kids offers keen insights on behavior and financial issues. John Whitcomb's use of the notions of capitation and budgeting are at the heart of the financial dynamics of the healthcare system. The manner in which they have been adapted to personal finance is imaginative and very appropriate for parents teaching their children to manage their finances.

> —*Mark Covaleski, PhD, Professor of Healthcare Financial Management, University of Wisconsin-Madison*

Capitate Your Kids provided us with a clear guide to introduce our children to the skills and responsibilities they need to live within a budget. It offered helpful lessons to teach them how to get their money's worth and live within their means.

> —*Flip Troiano, M.D., and Aaria Troiano, Lecturer, University of Wisconsin-Milwaukee*

I have been using the *Capitate Your Kids* system for over two years with my 13-year-old and 16-year-old. Not only have I saved money, but I have also eliminated the begging and whining. This system is better than any economics class. I have no doubts about their ability to manage money when they leave home.

> —*Kathy Ledvina, VP for Managed Care Contracting, Aurora Healthcare*

My wife and I have begun applying some of the basic principles outlined in John Whitcomb's book *Capitate Your Kids* with our 12-year-old daughter. It is a joy to see her embrace and learn money management through goal setting and budgeting. She truly appreciates the trust we have shown in her and the independence/responsibility that accompanies it. Best of all, we have had no fights over money in almost a year!

> —*Jeff Stephenson, Director of Care Management, Aurora Healthcare*

John Whitcomb has combined humor, sound effects, and common sense into a short guide that goes long on how to teach your kids the true value of money.

> —*John Burkhalter, International Trade Account Manager, GE Medical Systems Washington, D.C.*

CAPITATE
Your Kids

Teaching Your Teens Financial Independence

THEY do the work, YOU save money!

By

Dr. John E. Whitcomb

Foreword by Bob Potter
Former Host, Minnesota Public Radio's *Sound Money*

popcorn
PRESS ™

Cover and Text Design by Georgene Schreiner
Edited by Carolyn Kott Washburne
Back Cover Photo by Photography by Jacquie

04   03   02   01   5   4   3   2

ISBN 0-9702518-2-3
Library of Congress Catalog Card Number: 00-107061

First Printing October 2000
Printed in the United States of America

Published by Popcorn Press, a division of Printstar Books
Milwaukee, Wisconsin

5630 N. Lake Drive, Milwaukee, WI 53217
414-906-0600 • e-mail:pbpub@execpc.com

Affiliated Publishers in
Milwaukee • Denver • Vancouver, B.C.

Dedication

To my parents, Bill and Dorothy Whitcomb, who believed in their children, always trusting that we could and would succeed, and that the measure of all our successes would be what we were able to give back.

Acknowledgments

This book is a creation of kindness.

Mary Ihde, working next to me in my day job, patiently heard idea after idea and gave gentle encouragement and patient suggestions. Jeff Stevenson kept insisting I write my ideas down. Mark Covaleski, Professor of Managerial Accounting at the University of Wisconsin-Madison, took my manuscript and gave me great encouragement at the beginning when the writing was its most raw. Flip Troiano read very raw versions and just assumed it would get done. John Burkhalter gave great feedback. Linda and Dave Schnable and Tom and Kim Larson believed I could finish the book. Kathy Ledvina came up with the name. Beth Meyer gave me the resolve to trust my instincts. My special gratitude goes to my cousin Joanne Tenaglio who spent hours and hours designing my superb Web site.

Many friends shared their families' experiences with humor and insight. Mike Hargarten showed a clear instinct for the love of his family and how kindness works in addition to consequences. Pat Green told me story after story about her "Capitated Kids." I beg forgiveness from the dozens of families whose ideas and encouragement are part of this book but who are not mentioned here by name. They tried out the Capitation Method, and wrote and e-mailed me with their successes and ideas. I trust that the skills their kids learned are some token of my gratitude.

Chris Reardon nourished the first edition as a friend and mentor. She is an editor for any new writer wanting to create a book. Popcorn Press is a special publishing company whose publisher, Susan Pittelman, produced a book any author would be proud of. Christopher Franks, an intern at Popcorn Press from the University of Wisconsin-Milwaukee, painstakingly reviewed every page, every reference, and every dangling participle, making the chapters hang together rather than separately. His care and tact this early in his career bodes well for many future authors. Georgene Schreiner made the text come alive with her caring and patient design and revisions. And Carolyn Kott Washburne proved that a great editor can take a good book and make it great.

But it all started with Holly, my spouse, my friend, and my creative conscience. She taught me, by gentle example, to take "artist's dates"—time apart to express my creative side, the spirit of the divine within each of us. And with my children, who rolled their eyes each time I began another Fiscal Fable, and patiently put up with the ideas and experiments of a restless and loving father. They are in this book more by allegory than by fact. I owe much gratitude to them.

CAPITATE Your Kids

CONTENTS

As the creator and host of the *Sound Money* program for fifteen years (1985 to 2000), I have received many calls from parents who want to help their children develop a sense of financial responsibility. *Capitate Your Kids*, by Dr. John Whitcomb, is by far the best "kids and money" product I've come across.

Far too many students come out of college many thousands of dollars in debt. They take on that debt without a clue about what's involved in paying it back. Some will have kids of their own in college before their own college loans are repaid. The time to begin teaching kids about serious money management is in the teen years, and that's exactly what *Capitate Your Kids* does. The premise of the book is that teens need to be taught how to be financially responsible. This is something not taught in school, and it's a critical life skill! And the best way to teach children is through their own experiences, in the safety of their homes, and under the guidance of their parents—parents who have a clear vision of what they want for their children.

Capitate Your Kids gives you the tools to make that vision concrete. You will read about teaching your teens to make budgets, anticipate large expenses, plan for rewards, and see the planning played out. The final chapters present a step-by-step methodology for gradually increasing the level of responsibility your teens assume and the sophistication of their financial tools.

You will also laugh along with Whitcomb as he describes his own and his teenagers' foibles. Who among us has not seen carefully planned budgets come apart under the strain of the unexpected events of everyday life? At great expense we have learned how to dig out and carry on. Whitcomb's "Fiscal Fables" will help you to incorporate your own experiences into the process so that your teens can learn from your mistakes as well as from their own.

But it doesn't stop there. *Capitate Your Kids* presents far more than the details of teaching kids how to manage money. It embraces the values of hard work, careful planning, charitable giving, and living within your personal means.

Whitcomb writes in a voice that is compassionate yet clear-headed, and he helps empower young people instead of dumbing them down at a time when they are yearning for more freedom and responsibility. This book will help you to help your children become hardworking and productive, generous and kind. You and your children will be grateful.

Bob Potter
Former Host, Minnesota Public Radio's *Sound Money*
Senior Advisor, JNBA Financial Advisors, Bloomington, Minnesota

HISTORICAL ROOTS

Money, in one form or another, has been around ever since human beings found that cowry shells from the beach could be traded for a bunch of coconuts. Only in the last generation have the number and complexity of financial transactions multiplied in our lives. Children who grew up with a stay-at-home mom in a home defined by home-cooked meals, home gardens, and local neighborhoods did not need much more than an allowance. The advent of families with two working parents, neither of whom cooks, sews, or stays at home much, in conjunction with spreading suburban neighborhoods and advertising-driven consumption, means that teens today have a dizzying array of financial options and responsibilities before them.

Children growing up in the fifties and sixties only needed money to spend on Saturdays. But children today have to carry money every day to buy milk at lunch, to call home in case they need to be picked up, to pay for extra expenses at school, and on and on. Members of today's households hardly ever sew their own clothes, pack their lunches, grow beans and tomatoes in a garden to can for winter, or entertain themselves by making their own toys. We all have to shop, every day. We all have to manage money, every day.

Furthermore, in the past one hundred years, our American society has developed a remarkable change in the way we care for our elderly. We don't. Instead of living with our children until we die in our fifties and sixties, as our great-grandparents did, we retire and live for decades beyond retirement in living arrangements remote from our children. To do that, retirees need financial resources independent from their children's—resources they must accumulate over a lifetime.

The extent to which these societal shifts are unprecedented, as well as unanticipated, is best indicated by the current fix our Social Security system is in. Fifty years ago, when the system was started, no one anticipated our elderly living as long as they do. When will tomorrow's retirees begin to learn the habits of lifetime accumulation of resources if not in their youth?

So it is only in the past few generations that we have developed such a pressing need for teens to become financially savvy. In this book I share with you a method that teaches you how to imbue your children with financial savvy while they are still living at home. Habits started at an early age imprint and set the stage for long-term success. It is a method my family learned by serendipitous trial and error over three generations. Children in America today cannot afford to risk serendipity gone wrong. They need to learn how to confidently manage their own financial affairs, live within their means, and plan thoughtfully for their future.

I believe that children learn from their parents by example and by story. Throughout history stories that represent fundamental truths have been passed on from parent to child. Within your own family many stories about your past experiences have already been told that your children love to hear. In this book about money management I call those stories "Fiscal Fables." Here is my own family's Fiscal Fable.

My mother's parents went to India as missionaries in the early 1920s to establish a school of agricultural engineering in the city of Allahabad in northern India. Both college graduates, they sent my mother away to boarding school for six or seven months a year from an early age. My grandmother, Clara Vaugh, had a strong belief in the independence of women, a radical concept in the twenties. While her husband was off making plows and pumps appropriate to rural India, my grandmother was teaching village women to weave multicolored baskets that became internationally known and propelled a community of low-caste, illiterate women to financial independence. Financial independence for women was of no small importance in my grandmother's family.

With her daughters away in boarding school, Clara decided to make them financially literate, just as she had done with her village women. To accomplish that, she wanted her daughters to have funds over which they could practice responsibility. Starting when my mother was in eighth grade living in a British boarding school in the foothills of the Himalayas, my grandmother sent her a check each month from which she was to pay all her expenses. That check was not just a token sum. It was the entirety of the financial support that the Presbyterian mission board sent to their missionaries as a salary supplement for the care of dependent children. My mother got "her own money."

My mother often tells the story of having her first check come in the mail. She was so proud that she hid it in the most special place of all, her Bible. However, despite her being the child of missionaries, her Bible was not the most frequently used of her possessions. When she needed her money, she was not able to find that check. She had to turn her whole dorm room upside-down before she accidentally knocked her Bible over and found the precious piece of paper.

Between 1937 and 1942 my mother would go to the school cashier faithfully each month with her check in hand to pay her tuition and room and board. She was also responsible for buying her own clothes. This involved purchasing cloth and taking it to a tailor, who would measure her and then duplicate items she pointed out from a worn Sears catalog. With what was left after her expenses she "kept out four annas each week for allowance, just like all the other kids," she reported to me when I asked where she got the inspiration to start us on our own money. "We would put one anna in the offering at church, and the other three were for snacks."

My father was the child of medical missionaries in India. Same boarding school. Same concept. Same time. My parents were classmates as children and as teens.

"Lots of the kids' parents did it. They were so out of touch with their parents when they were away in boarding school, their parents sort of just had to. There was no other way," my mother explained. "Your father was quite the businessman in school. He would take his money and go to the bazaar and buy brown sugar, butter, and peanuts, and make peanut brittle and sell it. He would get his little kerosene stove all pumped up down behind the gym and get the sugar to a nice soft ball. It was very good candy that the other kids bought. He had a regular little store going, selling soap and all sorts of supplies."

When I attended the same boarding school from 1957 to 1969 and my parents were agricultural and library science missionaries in India, I was similarly expected to manage my own finances. My siblings and I were expected to be self-sufficient enough to handle our own expenses, buy our own clothes, and budget for our own special occasions. We lived away from home for four months at a time. Three days of tedious train travel separated us from parental oversight. The mail could take a week in the mid-sixties, and long-distance telephones were merely an abstract concept.

I paid the school bursar each month for tuition, and paid for travel home when school was out. I remember very clearly thinking that my shoes could make it at least another six months if the *mochi* (shoemaker) could get a new sole to stick to the two layers of patches already on the shoes, which I polished three times a week.

Each week I saved money at the post office with a passbook account. When I was in ninth grade, my older sister and I used that money to pay for a special trip to South India. Traveling by ourselves at ages fourteen and seventeen, one thousand miles from home in a part of the country where we couldn't speak the language, didn't bother us at all. We took for granted we had all the skills we needed to travel and make it home safely.

Since that time my three siblings and I have each acquired an average of ten years of post–high school education, all of it on borrowed or earned money. We were able to do so because it became second nature to each of us to plan for the long term, to feel comfortable with financial concepts, and to become used to handling large amounts of money, of which only a small part could be discretionary. We were trusted and entrusted with money from an early age. We practiced being responsible. And that responsibility is what breeds success. Not the overwhelming overnight financial success of athletic superstars, but the long-term success of hard work, careful planning, and sound middle-class values. These values are what the best of America is about, and what your kids can learn as well. That is my wish for you.

John E. Whitcomb

John E. Whitcomb

A FISCAL FABLE

D o you enjoy shopping with your kids? Or are you exhausted by their begging, whining, and nagging? Perhaps you find your temper a little bit stretched when you give in to one request and they try to leverage more from you by respond- ing with an alternative demand that costs twice as much. Money just seems to evaporate out of your wallet whenever your kids express their needs. You might be feeling that your spending on your children is way out of control.

If these are not issues for you, this may not be the book for you. But for the rest of us, the nagging, the begging, the frustration, and the expense seem endless. This book is about changing all that, doing it smarter, wiser, and—in the end—much cheaper.

Remember your last trip with small children to a grocery store? The assaults on your sense of responsible decision making never quit. Your kids circle out from your grocery cart like predators after prey, coming back with the products of their hunt, begging, "How about a box of CocoSmochos?" They cost six bucks a box, you note. Every item they

1

find comes directly from the most recent ads they've seen on television, never from the bargain bin.

After saying "no" fifty times, you feel your karma is better off without the stress of your kids helping you. Leave the irresponsible overconsumers at home—you're buying bran flakes.

But when these same kids get a little older, are they ready to go to college on their own? Have they learned how to delay gratification long enough to avoid the fast-paced impulse consumption of the new millenium? You'd like to believe that your children know how to make the right decisions. You want to feel confident that they know how to live within their means, planning for a remote future beyond next Saturday. Instead, do you fear that if you put money into a Uniform Gift to Minors fund in their names, they might buy a Jeep Grand Cherokee on their eighteenth birthday? If so, this is your book.

I am about to share with you the method of financial education my family has worked out in collaboration with our kids. My purpose is to show you the process that will enable you, in turn, to teach your kids the financial decision making that is in sync with your family values. You will be teaching your kids good cultural values about respecting their elders, respecting your faith tradition, contributing to society, and investing in their own future. Along with this you and your kids can learn how to share financial planning and goal setting together and establish a relationship between your family's cultural values and the management of money.

In the end, money is just money. It is a tool, a medium of exchange. It isn't the be-all and end-all. But the fact remains that people need money to live in modern society.

Once your kids learn to handle money competently, they can get on with the rest of their lives.

Living competently with money means learning how to live within one's means. Frugality and delayed gratification can be justified in the context of trading off immediate gratification for better gratification down the road. To accomplish such abstract and remote goals requires confidence in an inner sense of planning and restraint on impulses. It requires resisting the temptation to live by the yardsticks of status and consumerism, which our advertising culture demands, and living instead by internal yardsticks of contentment with our current state so we can focus on what will come along later.

Your kids should finish their teenage years with a sense that their parents trusted them and that they learned to trust themselves. The arena of money and money management is a wonderful laboratory in which to practice concrete examples of your trust and belief in them, even when they mess up. If they can leave home with the confidence that they have learned the necessary money management skills, you will feel you have been a successful parent, at least in one meaningful way.

Our culture has substantial taboos against talking about the values we hold most private: our sex lives and our money. This book is not about your kids' sex lives—we are still looking for that book. This book is about how to learn a collaborative, successful approach to raising your children to manage money effectively.

It goes without saying that managing money competently is always the cheapest way to go. Good money management is also learning how to control one's need to spend and being happy with that self-control. The methods you are about to discover will save you money and leave you with the conviction that you did it right. There is a way through the dark woods of those teenage years. In fact, once you see your kids getting the hang of managing money responsibly, the process gets to be almost fun.

WHAT IDEAS ARE WE WORKING WITH HERE?

Capitate! What does that mean? Actually, the idea is pretty easy. A capitated contract is one in which a fixed amount of money is paid for a product or service. The party responsible for the outcome of the service can get to the goal in whatever way he or she sees fit. The party paying for the service is guaranteed that the cost is agreed upon and will not change.

The federal government calls it "block grants"—giving a chunk of money to the states for a certain designated service and letting the states handle it as they see fit. You call it making ends meet, balancing the checkbook, getting by. You have a certain amount of money that has to match a certain set of needs and desires.

The term "capitated" is used in healthcare to define a contract in which doctors and hospitals are paid a fixed amount each month to care for a population of patients. In health care, capitation shifts the responsibility for maintaining wellness to doctors and hospitals.

Do these ideas fit into your family? Sure. Your children need to learn how to handle money. They are eager to do it. I am about to show you how to work out a plan for a fixed amount of money (a budget) that is to be paid to your teens for a specific responsibility, such as keeping themselves clothed and groomed. They are being "capitated" for the service of taking care of themselves in the contextual values of your family. How they spend, how they save, what they give to charity are all important cultural values within your family. Learning how to do each of these requires practice, example, and explicit direction. Which comes first? Do you want your kids to give first, save second, and spend third? Or is that just an ideal and you are not quite sure how to get them there? This book is intended to get you there.

Capitation leaves you out of the conflicts that arise when you try to take care of your kids without their consent.

Such conflicts often make you want to "decapitate" them and serve them up on a platter. They probably are thinking the same about you.

Maybe we can leave the definition of capitation as simply that— putting a head back on your teen, just when you were not sure if he or she had one. The genius of the concept is that your teens are putting their own heads on their own growing shoulders. They do all the work.

American society has no shortage of messages about the idea that money is the universal medium of exchange, the lubricant of social interaction. Your kids want to get in on the action. They want to be treated as adults and to have the resources that adults have. You want them to be competent at money management, and in doing so, you want them to practice the critical skills of saving and giving as well—the values you want your kids to have as adults. Without the skills of daily management the ideals of saving and charity are just dreams.

Another fact is that the longer one goes to school, the better one's earning potential becomes. As kids get to their early teens, the education road ahead looks as if it's light-years long. They feel they haven't got much control over an awful lot of it. (How badly do you want your kids to go to college? How about a graduate degree after that? Well, that could amount to twelve years after eighth grade—double their current age!) When I look at unemployment rates based on levels of education and I see eight to ten percent for high school grads and one-half to one percent for graduate school grads, I want my children to have as much education as they can get . . . and afford.

Where in all that learning process do you see your kids learning how to handle their monthly budget? Where do you see them being taught how to gauge how much they can borrow to pay for school? Who is out there showing them how to make ends meet, convincing them that money does not grow out of ATMs, or warning them that credit cards are expensive loans? Is anyone teaching them that delayed gratification can have tremendous rewards?

You do not see much, if any, financial learning going on in our schools. Kids leave home after high school on their way to life with a variety of aspirations that have financial implications. Kids aspire to become highly educated in order to get good jobs and be well paid, but they do not have the tools to manage their income, regardless of how modest it may be. Buying a house requires planning and saving. Even the purchase of a first used car takes a fair amount of thought. With current school instruction our kids have learned few financial tools to help put all those plans together. Even worse, by the end of high school we expect our kids to know all those attitudes and skills we learned by our own trial and error, such as overspending and then having to dig ourselves out of a deep debt hole. We watch helplessly as every credit card company in America showers our kids with offers of easy credit.

A bad time to learn these lessons is during the years of advanced education after high school, because students overwhelmed by financial stress are more likely to drop out. Yet school represents the very means on which their opportunity to pay off their debt rests. Your teens need as much education as they can get. Society needs them to become as educated as they can be. We all benefit from their educations. To stay educationally motivated, they have to learn to handle money before they get to college.

The values we are dealing with in these pages start with simple concepts. Your kids need to learn how to handle money before and during high school. We've settled that. Even though that's not the only lesson they need to learn, if they can get that one down pat, they've got the context for working on many others.

The goal is for your kids to become competent at the management of their small universe of money so they can focus on the big stuff such as education, lasting and caring love relationships, and stewardship of this planet.

They might even get savvy enough to let their creative side blossom and learn money management well enough to discover how to really make money and become entrepreneurs. This has been the real genius of our American culture—our ability to produce an entrepreneurial drive and vision in our economy. To continue to realize that genius, we need every generation to pick up the values of risk and reward that start with the very basics—one's own universe of responsibility and reward.

So, what are the values in relationship to money that this book talks about? Let's list the ten of them.

Value Number One: Letting Go of Control and Trusting Your Kids

This one starts with you. You have the power and control. You have the money. For your kids to learn, you need to let go of your control over "their money," the money you would spend on them anyway. Make the intentional decision to transfer control to your kids' hands. You need to believe that you have good kids who are just dying to have you trust them.

Thus, Value Number One starts with you and ends with you.

Control in your hands is the source of conflict and is a way of keeping your dependents dependent. Unfortunately, you won't get what you want if you go down that road—you will just get rebellion and frustration and lots of immature behavior to further justify your need for more control. That starts a downward spiral of dysfunction. Don't go there!

The flip side of letting go of control is trust. Trust is a much more nurturing frame of reference. You need to make the argument in your mind that you want to trust your kids. Decide to make a forum in which they can prove to you that they are trustworthy. This means they have to have something of value with which to be trusted. What else is more important to them than the resources you spend on them and your trust that they will spend those resources well?

This principle of trust and self-governance has far wider implications than those found in this book. The modern, well-managed American corporation is composed of self-reliant, independent, self-managed work teams that are responsible for their own destinies. Teaching your children a similar model of self-reliance and personal responsibility will also go far in making them well accustomed to succeeding in the dizzying world of the new American workplace. That aside, the principles of capitation will help you get your kids off first base. Trust them, and they will blossom with self-confidence.

Value Number Two: Learning Happens from Mistakes for Which There Are Consequences

You learned by making mistakes. The trial-and-error method works. You probably look at many of your youthful misadventures as "learning experiences" instead of calling them bald-faced botches. And you did learn from them. Give your kids the same opportunities. Just as you send your kids to school to solve tough math and science problems, give them the opportunity to work on rigorous financial responsibility problems at home. When I smoked my first cigarette behind the school in one huge deep inhalation, I upchucked into the bushes for five minutes immediately thereafter. I learned from that. Well, after the third time.

If the best learning happens from connecting behavior to consequences, a good time to give your kids the opportunity to learn is when the cost is in a range you can handle. Starting with small responsibilities establishes the tools your teens need. Once those tools are in place, your teens can be entrusted with larger circles of responsibility. The alternative is to wait for your kids to discover the consequences of poor judgment and lack of planning the first semester they are off at Big Bucks U. "Dad, you know that $4,000 you gave me last month for living expenses . . . ?"

By starting your kids early on a process over which they have control, you allow them to make little mistakes over smaller universes of responsibility in a place that is safe—your home—over issues that are not vital to their immediate survival. Heat, light, medical care, and a stocked fridge are necessary to their immediate survival. Their learning to handle money responsibly for nonvital items allows you to keep safe control over vital items and medical bills. Learning the tools of money management in the safety of home gives teens the skills they need before it's time to go off to BBU, where they become responsible not just for their discretionary allowance, not just for their clothes and tooth-paste, but also for their food and shelter.

Value Number Three: Learning to Plan over Long Periods

Your kids need reliable, monthly, safe money for them to spend. Money that can't be taken away. Money that's there for them to make mistakes with. (They will.) There are consequences if they mess up, but not so dire as to be dangerous. The money's there every month, in big enough doses to be meaningful—and for purposes that intensely interest them.

We are talking about control and planning here: putting your kids in control of a small part of their lives. You let go of control over them. They get control. It happens every month, but never all at once.

This means they have to plan ahead. They have to save up for the big stuff. They have to go lean during the saving period. They have to plan, wait, and be rewarded for waiting. Planning means making a budget. Budgets do work. Making a budget means having a handle on the "big picture." They delay gratification now to get something better down the road. And when your kids do it right, they will have extra left over for which they have bonus choices.

The only reason to delay gratification now is that it makes the future better. Being able to delay gratification is a critical life skill. Enduring the discipline of pain now leads to much better rewards later. A little more pain means a lot more reward. Delaying gratification is not learned in one fell swoop. Kids need to practice it at little levels on little projects.

Then college doesn't feel so long. Graduate school doesn't feel endless. For every year of school completed past high school, income goes up 15 percent. That is reward for delayed gratification in its purest form.

How much do you spend for a pair of sneakers for your teen? Current culture demands they spend about $200 a pair. That is the status symbol du jour—expensive sneakers. You want them to feel good about having a pair that cost $40, the functional kind that are just as good as the more expensive ones. You want your teen to make the connection that the $160 they save on sneakers can be used for something else. Being frugal has rewards. But you, the parent, cannot make that value decision for your teen. Your teen has to learn to feel that value internally.

Your job changes from micromanagement over a budget to supervision over values and opportunities. You stop being the budget cop and start being chauffeur. "You want to go clothes shopping? Sure, I'll take you. How much money have you got in your account this month?"

You stop being the naysayer and start being the true leader in the family. You establish cultural values. Saying to your children that you expect and empower them to budget and plan ahead says that delayed gratification is an important cultural value that leads to great rewards. They will pick up on that value and learn to treasure it.

Value Number Four: Fairness

The Capitation Method works when you act on the principle of teaching your kids to spend for themselves what you would normally have spent on them. We are not talking about saving money in the immediate sense. The intent here is not to do this project for cheap. If you plan a budget carefully enough with your child, you should spend exactly what you would have anyway for your family's expectations and income. The intent is to be fair and successful. Say to yourself, "I want my child to succeed, and I am not going to rip my kid off." Your success comes not in saving money in the short term but in creating a state of mind that living contentedly within your means is the key to financial independence.

11

The temptation exists to be reactive to irresponsible, spoiled teens and create a budget that will punish them for their profligate ways. That won't work. All parents of teens have, at some point, muttered under their breath the vow to ground their offspring for the remainder of their lives, prematurely shortened though that may be. Such a punitive approach is the inevitable outcome of fruitless fighting over control. If control issues are released, fights don't happen. Success depends on identifying and rewarding positive behaviors, not punishing errors. Your job as a parent is creating culture, not petty rules with punitive consequences.

The truth behind this principle is that once your kids feel responsible and fairly treated, they will learn to live happily within their means, and that is much cheaper for you. In the long run the method I advocate here saves you bundles. Your kids develop an attitude of solving problems within the means at their disposal, recognizing that doing so—planning, budgeting, waiting, and saving—will result in successful outcomes. Living contentedly within the limited resources one has is the first key step to life-long contentedness. Not learning that lesson is the first step to keeping up with the Joneses, and that is the first step to lifelong money struggles. To start, you have to create the attitude with your kids that you are being fair.

Value Number Five: Build on Your Success

Kids learn fast. You can start with some simple ideas and build from there. The concept of imprinting is to create a behavior by introducing it at just the right developmental time in a growing being's maturation process. You want your kids to be imprinted with responsibility and successful money management skills at the age at which they need to start making their own decisions. The rebelliousness of teenagers is the best indicator of their insistence that they want to make their own decisions. Lesson Plan One (pp. 101–108) gives you a step-by-step budget process for a limited universe of responsibility starting at age eleven or twelve: clothes. Clothes are a good place to start because they are so immediate in terms of use and need, as well as in demand for peer issues.

Once your children have learned the idea of designing and calculating a Clothing Budget, they should be given the responsibility of managing that budget. When they have developed the skill set for managing their clothing expenditures, introduce a more inclusive budget. Once that budget is developed, build on your success and give them control of it. Ages thirteen to fourteen are good ages for them to design and start gaining control over a gradually larger budget universe.

Once your children have learned the budgeting process and have some control over it, how about having them learn a couple of different methods by which they can demonstrate their control? By that I mean you can start with a cash basis of transactions for an early budget and then move to more sophisticated methods of transactions, such as a debit card and then a checkbook. Once your children are old enough for a driver's license, they are ready for their own checkbooks. Once they have their checkbooks, it is time for them to learn to pay more of their own expenses.

Learning in small steps works. As long as your children have the forum to make learning progressive and to continue to build on their prior successes, they have the foundation to go a long way.

An analogy can be made between progressive financial learning and progressive driver's ed. Over the last decade many states have recognized the inadequacy of driver's education for teenagers. (Did you know that a sixteen-year-old driver with the traditional, limited driver's education of five to ten hours of observed driving has approximately a 25 percent chance of having an auto crash in the first twelve months of driving?) Many states used to have very limited requirements for driving experience before teenagers were given the freedom of the road. Legislators in many states have responded to the terrible death rate among inexperienced teen drivers by drafting legislation to give graduated driving privileges.

Graduated driver's licenses are now being considered or have been enacted in the majority of states. Here again the principle of graduated learning that builds on earlier successes allows for stepwise learning, with concrete rewards for each new level of demonstrated responsibility.

The last section of this book, Contracts, includes a sample contract you can write with your teen for graduated driving privileges. It follows the same idea used by those states that have made it their legal format but is more restrictive because of grade-related rewards. In the sample contract your teenagers start driving with an adult supervising them for an extended period of time so they can experience a variety of driving conditions under the watchful eye of an adult and demonstrate mature attitudes and habits.

Consider your teenager's financial learning to be along the same lines. A step-by-step process builds on success in both the financial and the driving arenas of your teenager's life. The consequences of financial crashing are not quite so lethal as crashing an automobile, but—in the lifelong sense—learning to live within one's means is the key to secure financial independence. Safe driving down the financial highway of life requires graduated learning.

If these ideas are resonating so far, we are on a roll. You are getting the hang of it.

Value Number Six: Consequences Follow Behavior

There is nothing more potent than consequences that flow from behavior—without your being the person affecting those consequences. Handling their own money is a very real laboratory in which your teens can learn this principle.

Equally important is to make the reward one of the consequences. Most of the teens I talk to who have tried the Capitation Method say that what they like best is not having to "beg for stuff" they need and "being able to get what I want with what's left over." That's a built-in reward. A parent doling out a reward can be taken for granted. Teens earning their own rewards because their behavior is what led to the rewards is the basis for effective learning.

Concrete rewards are the tangible things you can buy by being frugal in one area and saving enough to buy something special in another. Abstract rewards soon follow. Your teen develops confidence in being able to budget, plan, save, wait, and carry out financial aspirations. If giving is an important value in your family, the abstract pleasure of having enough to give and share can be practiced again and again, and its own abstract internal rewards will take over.

Value Number Seven: Consumption Has to Match Income

Money does not grow on trees. Not a terribly new idea. How old were you when you learned it? The only way to really learn it is to bump up against it every month. Kids learn it best if they run out of money every month just like the rest of us do. You cannot learn this rule in a classroom. You cannot learn it in one month.

We are all a little like alcoholics when it comes to this lesson. Until we hit bottom hard a bunch of times, we are incredibly capable of denying the consequences of our actions. When your kids are the ones who engineer the hard landings time and time again, they remember clearly just how they got there. They cannot blame Mom and Dad—just themselves. They learn.

This is the "hard lesson" we want our kids to learn. Just as we want our children to learn challenging lessons at school, living within one's income is the challenging lesson to learn for financial independence. It has to be hard for it to be internalized. The only way to be secure is to learn to live on less than what you have.

Learning to live on less than what we have—and being content with that—is the first step to accumulating wealth. Over the course of a lifetime, any middle class family can become a millionaire family if it starts with a lifestyle of living within its income limits and saving the difference. This is not a complex concept; financial independence and self-reliance depend upon it.

To internalize that value, we need to bump up against limitations during our formative years and develop the emotional tools to feel good about navigating within the limits of what we have. Learning to feel okay about resisting expensive sneakers is the best way to learn to feel good about driving a safe, reliable car instead of an expensive import.

Resisting the desire to spend limited financial resources on status items such as expensive cars is the only way most of us can accumulate the wealth that allows us to afford other, much more precious values, such as freedom from financial worry, the pleasure of giving to worthy causes, and financial security in retirement.

Although this is a hard lesson, we humans become proud of ourselves when we learn hard lessons. We internalize them, build on them, and follow those hard-won principles for the rest of our lives.

Value Number Eight: Good Values, Not More Stuff

Schools do not teach this. As parents we are responsible for teaching our children our values. They learn our values regardless of our efforts; they learn by copying our actions. We create the dynamic of trust with our children when we set them off on a course of responsibility and independence. We are no longer the keepers of the details of their behavior; rather, we are framers of the bigger picture. We model trust and provide the opportunity for them to learn frugality and delayed gratification—all of which leads to what you really want your children to learn: a system of good values toward money.

By using the Capitation Method taught in this book, you are teaching the values of planning, delayed gratification, personal initiative, responsibility, frugality, and common sense. You can extend your expectations for your kids' use of money to include saving for the future and giving to charity.

Saving for the future is the key to long-term financial independence. Savings are achieved by living slightly below one's means and by feeling content with doing so. The accumulation that occurs is steady, long term, and reliable. A primary cultural concept that allows savings to occur is learning to make the choice between utility and prestige, value versus status. Our advertising-dominated, image-driven society tempts us to live for the moment, and it teaches us to consume for the purpose of prestige. Who is teaching the longer-term values if not us, parents? Most of us want our kids to learn to become financially independent, capable of accumulating wealth in the only way that really works for all of us—the hard way.

The Capitation Method allows you to impart your cultural values step-by-step, one little dose at a time, as outlined in detailed steps in the six Lesson Plans in the second-to-last-section of this book. Giving your kids responsibility to manage a bank account creates a reason to sit down every month when the bank statement arrives. At that time you can review issues that might otherwise not have arisen or been given a forum for discussion. Your kids can hear your stories of how you had your first financial learning experiences, your Fiscal Fables. Can you honestly tell your teen that you knew how to handle a checkbook when you graduated from high school, or were aware of what would happen to your credit rating if you did not pay your bills? (Be fair, your fable is meant to have a kernel of truth in it!) When you were in college, were you aware that using a credit card is the most expensive way of borrowing money? You are now. Do you have a reason to sit down with your kids every month and teach a little bit of what you learned by painful trial and error? The Capitation Method creates the framework in which those conversations can occur.

If you are in a control fight over money every month, your kids are much less likely to hear your words of wisdom as anything but nagging. They have no impetus to learn the ideas you are talking about because it is not a shared experience for them. Their natural teen rebelliousness will lead them to challenge you instead of learn from you. Challenge they probably must, to some degree. But learning from your experience is a wonderful alternative.

Value Number Nine: Saving, Giving, and Investing Take Practice

Learning to save is a skill that requires having resources to work with. The same with giving. Ditto for investing. Once children have learned the concept of being in control and looking beyond this coming Saturday, higher-order money management skills start falling into place. The Capitation Method creates the context in which such behaviors become meaningful.

As a parent you have to model charitable giving and saving for the future and for retirement. Your teens become your peers when they contribute to charity along with you. If they see you doing it, they will inherit your state of mind, your commitment to doing it. They will hear you saying the same phrases you heard from your parents. "The first 10 percent goes to charity, the second 10 percent is to pay myself, and the rest goes to the government." You heard that from your parents, didn't you? Say it to your kids. Practice it.

Your kids need to see you creating limits to spending because you believe in saving and charitable giving more than you believe in buying for status or prestige. They need to see you making such choices as spending $30 for a watch that works instead of $3,500. They need to see you buying a car that gets you safely from home to work for a reasonable cost instead of an expensive, racy sports car. They need to see you creating a voluntary environment of limits, imposed because you want to use your money for purposes other than impulse spending for prestige, and because you are committed to saving and giving first. If you do it, your kids will see it and copy you. Practicing it again and again on a monthly basis starts to build the attitudes and the internal rewards for responsible money management.

Value Number Ten: Values Are Not Money

Our materialistic society is focused on money, but as we all know, money does not buy happiness. Teaching our kids to control their money desires and to know what their values are gives them a leg up on being able to focus more clearly on what real values they want to build their lives around. The eternal battle between status symbols and sensible utility will be waged as long as there is a form of communication by which we can be bombarded with advertising. We want our kids to learn to clearly see the difference.

You can get your kids to that point while respecting their needs, celebrating with them their success in learning, watching them succeed, and not being too judgmental when they mess up.

The Method

With all those ideas in mind, what is the Capitation Method? It's very simple once you have the right attitude and vision.

- Start by creating a budget that works within your spending limits and family values.

- With a budget in hand for your kids to work with, give them a regular income stream every month from which they are responsible for an ever-increasing amount of their budgetary universe. They start with pocket money, then clothes, then sports equipment, school supplies, gifts, toiletries, haircuts, CDs, snowboards, phone bills, car insurance—and end up with the works. I mean the works: rent, food, insurance, gas money. That's how much responsibility your teens can learn to have.

- Consistently teach the Capitation Method. As your kids do the work, you have to keep your eye on the concepts and ideas you are trying to teach. Here is where the idea of the "Fiscal Fable" really comes into play. All the above values are too abstract for a teen to take seriously. You are dead serious, but must take a less overbearing approach to communicate to teens. You can impart those ideas with stories and anecdotes, otherwise termed "Fiscal Fables," from your childhood, or experiences you "heard at work" that have a hidden fiscal message. Your teens will listen to stories far more receptively than to sermons and lectures.

I remember in vivid detail the story related to me by my father of how much I could buy if I didn't smoke. He was just saying it in passing, as though it was unintentional. Now, as an adult, I know it wasn't. You are now the parent, the storyteller, the Fiscal Fabler. You must take every opportunity to relate Fiscal Fables to your teens while they are learning this method. That is how they will learn. Remember, it is your responsibility to pass on culture and values, not nag over the details.

A Suggested Timeline

Because each child is unique, establishing a precise and exacting timeline is both inappropriate and impossible. However, some developmental thresholds are universal and provide general guidelines for a timeline. It is common for many children to begin to recognize the influence of their peers around age twelve or thirteen. In seventh grade many children start to stretch their wings and acknowledge the universe outside their families with a desire to conform to peer-driven clothing norms. It's at this point that this book suggests that you, the parent, start the Capitation Method. A year of practice with the Clothing Budget transitions easily into the increased responsibility of using an ATM card. After enough practice with these tools and concepts, your teen will be ready for a larger, more inclusive universe of responsibility and privilege: the Global Budget. Age sixteen, or tenth grade, offers the driver's license rite of passage. That peculiar American transition creates the opportunity for using a checking account. The graduated transitions from the Clothing Budget to the Global Budget mesh well with the financial tools of an ATM card and a checkbook.

The purpose of this book is to offer a smorgasbord of tools and ideas for you to consider and then apply to your child. Some families will find the concept of a clear set of lesson plans useful; see the section on Lesson Plans if that is your ken. Some will enjoy the more abstract guidelines of this chapter. Some will appreciate the boundaries defined in the stories that follow and will learn best from those Fiscal Fables. My hope is that each family will find something in these pages that resonates and makes the Capitation Method work for them.

The right timeline and tools are the ones that work for your child, under your loving care, in a way that matches your family's values, resources, and traditions. You can help transform your child into a teenager who has the tools of adulthood well in hand, so that leaving home for the larger world is only one more step confidently taken. By the time your kids leave home, they can be managing a monthly checkbook, using a credit card responsibly, and paying for all their expenses, even their rent—which comes back to you. (And if they stay too long, the rent can go up.)

You will be proud! And so will they.

CHAPTER TWO

WHAT IS THE RIGHT AGE TO START
AND WITH HOW MUCH?

When do you start reading to your children? When do you start saying prayers at their bedside? When do you expect them to do chores on their own? Intuitively you have an answer to all those questions. You know your children.

The most reliable answer to the question of when to start teaching your children to manage money is when the seat of your pants says it feels right. I think the connection between work in the home and money management should start being made as early as possible.

For example, you may expect your children to help with walking the dog, cleaning their rooms, changing their sheets, washing their clothes—in other words, whatever you find your children capable of doing. You probably give them their pocket money when their tasks are done. From ages four to ten this rule works pretty well: your kids do need you to be the boss and benevolent dictator. No chores, no pocket money. Behavior and reward demonstrate the alignment of real-world actions and consequences. In the year 2000 I think the range of one dollar a week for each year of age is about as high as one needs to go. Six dollars a week for a six-year-old should be enough to model some management of spending money, saving money, and giving money.

Money should not be the only consequence of good behavior. There should also be some connection between behavior and privileges. "You can play outdoors after all your clothes are picked up and your bed is made." With both privileges and money associated with responsibility, children learn to connect the two and see each as part of the natural order of things. Money and responsibility go hand in hand, as does earning the right to have some rewards for one's work.

Tasks that can be added to the list of responsible family chores need not be limited to milking the cows, herding the sheep, and baling the hay. Walking the dog and taking out the garbage are typical examples of family chores in suburban America. In our family we chose to focus on the responsibilities of caring for oneself and being respectful to the larger family.

"Please do your laundry and put it away before any weekend privileges," is pretty standard in our home. We expect our children to make their own school lunches before going to bed and to make their beds before going to school. Picking up after themselves before friends can come over is routine. Everyone gets a dishwashing night; everyone gets a turn at shoveling snow. Doing one's share of routine home maintenance is respectful behavior toward everyone in the family. Practicing kindness toward family members is also being respectful.

Those are all good behaviors to start practicing in the years before age ten. Age ten is about the earliest to begin the Capitation Method. That's the age at which children start being conscious of their clothing and what their peers are wearing. We've discovered, however, that starting at age twelve is better. Until then keeping a budget seems more like a game to keep Mom and Dad happy than serious planning. On the other hand, some of our friends who have tried the Capitation Method report an occasional child with very focused attention to detail and a strong need for independence before age twelve.

Our two children were ages ten and thirteen when we said, "Let's start the idea of a budget for your clothes." We started with clothes because we had only limited opportunities to go shopping, and when we did shop, the kids were always three sizes larger than they had been just a few months before.

You have probably noticed this phenomenon. You say to your children, "So let's buy everything you need and get it over with." Five shirts go into the cart, four pairs of pants, a jacket, and a new pair of tennis shoes. That can add up to $300 in one sweep through the department store. And four months later you hear, "I haven't got any clothes I like!" Investigation of the closet finds three new shirts, still in their store wrappers, never worn, and now too small. The jacket was lost somewhere during soccer practice, and the shoes are worn out.

"Mom, I need another jacket because last year's is way too small." Grrrrrrr.

There are well-known authors who state they can clothe their kids for $25 a year by using garage sales only. But that requires finding and looking through a hundred garage sales a year. We didn't garage sale shop. Many families do not have the luxury of spending their summer Saturday mornings working the garage sale scene. For those of you who do, think of that as part of your "imprinting" on your kids. Take them out on a few adventures and see what pops up. Many clothing items at garage sales are being sold for a dollar, little kids' items for less. Make the connection between applying a little initiative to finding adventure and finding a bargain. Garage sale shopping reinforces the value that inexpensive items (such as outgrown shirts still in their original packaging) can be found with some resourcefulness, and that doing so is a strong alternative value to simply buying based on the latest fashion. Your enthusiasm, excitement, and pleasure at finding a good bargain are infectious. Some day the rewards of bargain-hunting will come home to roost.

When we started our children's budgeting process, instead of spending the time and effort to garage shop, we set a 1995 clothing budget for each child at $800. The deal was that we would keep to that limit, and at the end any money left over was theirs.

It turned out that $800 was not enough in suburban, upper-Midwest America. When you have to buy for ninety-five degrees in the summer and twenty degrees below in the winter, a four-season wardrobe for growing children requires more clothing than we had anticipated.

Well, we got ten months into the year and ran out of the projected budget. Our son and daughter liked the idea a lot and thought $800 apiece was Fort Knox. But it wasn't. By the end of the year they were wearing completely worn-out shoes. Winter jackets at $100, two sets of sports shoes, a sweater, a sweatshirt, five or six pairs of jeans, gloves, boots, T-shirts, all in two sizes—you know the drill.

Our initial method of deciding the amount for a clothing budget was the try-it-out-and-see-where-you-fumble method. It can work for you, too, but it is sloppy. By having to give in later, you probably lose some of the value of having a realistic goal to stick to. You also lose the opportunity to model for your children the making of a budget by keeping track of expenses.

But that year did show us that we were on the right track. We knew right away we had stumbled onto something because our kids immediately began comparison shopping. They learned to look at price tags. Our son found good soccer shoes at the Play It Again Sports resale shop for half the price as at the soccer store. Our daughter discovered Kmart's shoes and decided she preferred three pairs of slip-on loafers at $10 to one pair of Nikes at $130. Our kids found winter jackets that were midrange in cost. They learned to wear jeans carefully.

And the begging stopped. Our relationship with our kids had a turn-around. Right away, we were operating on a partnership basis. "You want to go to Kohl's Department Store tonight and look at some shirts? Sure, I'll take you and pick up some groceries next door. It's your money."

If you want to just jump in like we did, you need to make some decisions about how you expect your kids to solve limits of spending. Most parents I speak to about the Capitation Method are initially shocked at the thought of $800 for a clothes budget—until they think about it. They quickly acknowledge its validity, in addition to the value of avoiding the control issues. For the year 2000, a range of $800 to $1,200 is realistic as a start. If you can take advantage of garage sales, thrift stores, or church hand-me-down sales, lower figures will work. For a daughter a slightly larger range of outfits might be desired that will probably require an additional increment. If you live in a milder climate, your figure might be a little lower.

Your budget does not need to be perfect. But you do need to start. Tell your kids, "Let's see how we do. The intent is not for you to fail, it is for you to have your own responsibility. I trust you to do your best. I will help you make decisions. If you run out of money, I will not let you go cold and uncared for. But I think you are old enough to start making some of your own decisions, and the only way is to start. I haven't got a magic formula, but I think you can make it work."

The basic message is, "I trust you. You are growing up. That is good. I am proud of you for it. I want you to succeed. I want us to work together to get us there together."

You will be very proud of how well your children respond to that affirmation. Try it. It feels good.

CHAPTER THREE

HOW DO YOU CALCULATE THE FIRST BUDGET?

One way to calculate your child's first budget is to take the ideas from the previous chapter and go with those rough numbers. In 2000, $1,000 a year for a teenager's clothing budget will be reasonably mid-range for a family that buys new clothes at standard department stores.

If you have the energy, you can also calculate a budget in other ways. The more work you put into planning a budget, the more your kid will learn from the mutual effort.

Calculating a budget works best if you can model it on how your family calculates its own budget. If your family sits down and makes projections that it later validates with a review of actual expenditures, use that same time and process with your child. Children learn the fastest from modeled behavior.

If you haven't built in your own planning and review process, this may be your opportunity to start. Your financial advisor will tell you that families who intentionally budget have a far greater likelihood of maintaining financial tranquillity. So get off your duff and do it. And include your kids while you're at it.

Let's look at the ways it can work.

Lesson Plan One (pp. 101–108) includes a detailed outline for teaching your children to budget in a step-by-step fashion. The outline is designed to guide parents to sit down each month and spend thirty minutes teaching their children financial smarts. The reason a monthly session is practical is that bank statements come once a month. However, outlines by themselves are pretty cold and do not teach judgment or context. The outline becomes useful once you, the parent, have digested the principles of this chapter.

Budget Method Number One

Plan ahead for a year before you anticipate giving your kids their own budgets. During that year observe and document your family's usual spending behavior. Save every check and credit card stub that represents your children's clothing over the course of that one year. Start in July, or in January, or on their birthdays—whatever annual event you can remember. Write the starting date on an envelope that you can use to hold your receipts. Recruit your kids to keep track as part of their own learning.

You may have some unusual events during the course of the year that will take some consideration. If you expect to move next year from New Orleans to Minneapolis (or some other geographical equivalent), add something for the change in climate. If your children are going to start a new sport, add an increment for sports equipment. If they have other special needs you anticipate, consider that as fair game to add, too. Annual planning gives you the opportunity to think of those special needs, and it gives you a reality check on how much you are actually spending.

While collecting receipts and totaling the costs, show these figures to your kids each month. Share with them the running totals. Ask them what they think, and if they think you are including enough. This is a great time to practice defining the different categories of clothing purchases—from underwear to shoes. Your kids will love to help. Have them add up the totals and design a table to show all categories in the budget. Remember, this is their first exposure to the ideas you are working with. Your kids will imprint on the method you use and will make it their own.

Projecting costs in this fashion requires a better-than-mortal attention span. Good intentions get frayed over Christmas, depressed in January, and so far behind by spring break that you may not be able to sustain the effort. If you are like the rest of us frail humans, give yourself a break. Try Budget Method Number Two.

Budget Method Number Two

This is not as elegant, but it is reality. Make a simple table such as the one that follows. Go to a local Sears, JCPenney's, Target, Kmart, Kohl's, or other store where you make your clothing purchases, or haul out the mail-order catalog. Write down the prices you find.

Budget Method Number Three

Least elegant, but most real. Read this book. Guess and get started. Real reality.

SAMPLE CLOTHING BUDGET FOR A BOY AGE 12

Underpants	8 pairs	@ $9–$11/3	$	30
Socks	12 pairs	@ $6/3	$	24
White T-shirts	4	@ $11–$14/3	$	36
Colored T-shirts	6	@ $13–$17	$	90
White shirt	1	@ $19–$30	$	29
Dress shirts	4	@ $19–$35	$	100
Sweatshirts	2	@ $19–$35	$	50
Pants	2 pairs	@ $22–$37	$	59
Jeans	3 pairs	@ $20–$35	$	100
Shorts	2 pairs	@ $13–$17	$	30
Sneakers	2 pairs	@ $39–$120	$	100
Sandals	1 pair	@ $2–$20	$	15
Dress shoes	1 pair	@ $35–$70	$	52
Winter jacket	1	@ $60–$110	$	75
Windbreaker	1	@ $19–$64	$	40
Winter gloves	1 pair	@ $5–$15	$	10
Scarf	1	@ $8–$20	$	10
Winter hat	1	@ $6–$19	$	15
Winter boots	1 pair	@ $39–$85	$	49
Sweater	1	@ $19–$30	$	29
Swimsuit	1	@ $17–$33	$	24

Total	$	**967**

SAMPLE CLOTHING BUDGET FOR A GIRL AGE 12

Underpants	12 pairs	@ $7–$10/3	$	32
Bras	6	@ $3–$12	$	40
Socks	12 pairs	@ $10/3	$	40
Pantyhose	4 pairs	@ $1.60–$3.90	$	10
T-shirts	6 pairs	@ $12–$17	$	87
Tops/blouses	6	@ $6–$12	$	54
Shirts	4	@ $16–$25	$	82
Skirts	3	@ $14–$25	$	60
Dresses	2	@ $22–$59	$	81
Jeans	5 pairs	@ $28–$39	$	150
Pants	2 pairs	@ $20–$33	$	53
Shorts	4 pairs	@ $15–$20	$	70
Dress pants	2 pairs	@ $16–$29	$	45
Dress shoes	2 pairs	@ $37–$54	$	91
Sneakers	2 pairs	@ $25–$47	$	72
Sandals	1 pair	@ $2–$90	$	20
Winter jacket	1	@ $19–$64	$	42
Windbreaker	1	@ $19–$48	$	31
Winter gloves	1 pair	@ $4–$17	$	10
Scarf	1	@ $9–$22	$	17
Winter hat	1	@ $11–$19	$	19
Winter boots	1 pair	@ $39–$72	$	60
Sweater	1	@ $14–$40	$	20
Swimsuit	1	@ $20–$45	$	30

Total   **$1196**

As you can see, these are not extravagant lists. In fact, you might just throw up your hands in amazement, turn to your exhausted spouse looking over your shoulder, and soften him or her up for a reality check by saying, "Honey, have you ever realized what we are spending on clothing for our kids?"

Of the many people to whom I have posed the question, "How much do you spend on your kids' clothes?" only one or two guessed that they spent $1,000 a year per child. But look at this list and contemplate those $180 high-top sneakers you bought last year that lasted four months before being left out in the rain. Add the jacket that was run over by the bleacher roller in the gym, and then add the twelve novelty T-shirts you paid $20 each for during the course of the year when you went to the county fair, the local theme park, and the mall novelty shop. Do you sense that no one in this country can afford to clothe a kid?

If your spouse is resistant to creating a higher budget for kids' clothing, rewrite the table leaving blanks for prices and quantities and have your spouse help you fill it out the next time you have a few free minutes at Nordstrom or any other very nice store. If that is where your family shops, your budget will be higher. A little shock therapy early in the process goes a long way toward later negotiations. I highly recommend it.

My kids spent one summer biking around to garage sales and picking up clothes for much less than what they would have paid at retail stores. But they were motivated veterans of capitated budget behavior. Garage sale sweatshirts often sell for two dollars or less. Of course, if you encourage this frugality by bargain hunting, be prepared for the "really cool leaf picker-upper" they bring home that they got for one dollar. "We can really rake the yard much faster with this, Dad!" Admire it, park it, and sell it when they head off for college.

If you follow Budget Method Number Two, which takes its figures from browsing price tags at a store or in a mail order catalog, make sure your children at least look over the list with you and change it to reflect their behavior or environment. Preferably include them on your trip to the store. Filling out their Clothing Budgets can be fun. They will most certainly help. They will also believe in the process once you have included them in it.

Belief is as important as the list itself.

Finally, recognize that your children are growing up and discovering new things and new horizons. You may not notice that your eighth grader could be going to a prom next year. What you need to talk about is that new desires and opportunities will come up during the course of the year and will need to be considered.

Maybe your child wants to take flute lessons, and you would like her to handle that money herself. Regardless of the care you put into designing your budget, something will arise to throw you off. This is just like real life. Think about how you might accommodate that curve ball. Again, the method of problem solving you demonstrate is modeling behavior for your children. If you want them to copy your behavior, try and be cool.

Next step, the contract.

CHAPTER FOUR

THE FIRST CLOTHING CONTRACT:
GETTING "THE CARD"

The world runs on contracts. A contract is simply an agreement between two parties that reflects promises for future behavior. We make contracts in our families all the time even though we may not recognize them as such. We tend to say, "What would you like to do this weekend, a movie? Okay, let's go!" That's a promise and a contract.

Because capitating your children promotes a set of behaviors that span a year or longer, you can add to the seriousness of the process by making a written promise between you and your children. That is a contract. And it's a good idea.

You don't have to be a lawyer for your kids to take their new financial arrangement more seriously when you write it down and list your expectations.

The Contracts section (pp.160–170) includes a sample of such a contract, along with other contracts I refer to in these pages. If you want to use that one, you can make the process easy.

The greatest value that comes from writing a contract is that each child sits down with you to plan the promises and responsibilities you both think will be involved.

You get a much more meaningful level of buy-in from your children if they are part of the planning and writing. They take the responsibilities much more seriously.

If you follow that route, be careful not to send your children off to do this work on their own. Writing a contract is too new a concept. Do it together as though you were holding a brainstorming session. You will know most of the ideas you want to include because of the lists you have made together as you planned their budgets.

Look over the sample contracts in the last section of this book. You may see some ideas you have not anticipated that you can bring to the brainstorming session. You can download these examples off of our Web site, www.capitateyourkids.com, and have a copy to word process.

Basic Elements of Your Contract

- Purpose
- Mom and Dad's responsibilities
- Child's responsibilities
- The list of all categories of clothing your child is responsible for purchasing on his or her own
- The amount of money you are going to turn over to your child each month
- How you will deliver the money
- Your own promise not to interfere while still providing transportation
- And, finally, the reward of getting the leftovers of any cash he or she does not spend

Contingency Elements

A few additional items are crucial to consider:

- What do you do with an unexpected expense?
- What happens if an expensive item is lost or stolen?

- What special needs are coming up this year? Is Uncle Mike getting married and asking your daughter to be a flower girl?
- How often do you both agree to sit down together and review your collective progress?
- What happens when your child loses his or her ATM card?
- What happens if your son or daughter withdraws cash below the minimum balance in the account?
- What happens if your son or daughter refuses to meet with you?

A little pomp and ritual added to the contract process can add dignity and seriousness. You can get a nice cover for your contract at the office supply store or make one with a word processor, using some fancy lettering. Photocopy or print copies for everyone involved. Make a ceremony of the signing. Watch how proud your child is. Officially hand over the first check or the ATM card as the finale. This signifies the child's having arrived at the threshold of adult financial responsibility. You are treating the child like a grownup, with respect. Cool!

Opening a Bank Account

The mechanics of getting a bank account opened for your child need to be addressed ahead of time. Many banks offer special accounts that give their customers an ATM card, provided the customer maintains a minimum balance. You, the adult, may need to make the down payment in the account that establishes the interest-free basis for the account. In an account that is used only for ATM withdrawals and has no check-writing privileges, banks usually require between $200 and $500 as a basis, or down payment. With this kind of account you can arrange for an additional amount to be transferred monthly from your checking account into that ATM account for your child's use.

Your child needs to be very clear on the fact that the money he or she is to use is very different from the base that you establish. The base money is yours, not to be spent. This should be itemized in detail in your contract.

I encourage a monthly transfer and deposit of funds. With the inevitable early spending behavior you will observe, offering limited funds at the beginning of the Capitation Method lowers your risk of financial meltdown.

It is entirely possible that the first few months will result in all the child's money and all your base line money being spent. Relief is only thirty days away with the next deposit. Although that might be enough to partially repair the overdrawn amount, it might take two or three months before the account gets back to base line.

Meanwhile, every month you will be sitting down together with your teen and going over the bank statement. Remember, no pain, no gain. You wanted tough lessons; this is the first of them.

The ATM card should come in duplicate, with a copy for you. You want to carefully save it, and have the PIN number tucked away as well. Another likelihood is that the ATM card will become bent or lost. Kids' wallets do not contain a multitude of cards that help keep the wallet rigid. As a consequence the card will get bent if it is alone in a wallet along with only a paper library card and a Record Club of America card. If the ATM card is carried free and open in a teenager's pocket, it will most likely be lost.

Make sure your contract spells out who gets to pay the bank fees for replacement cards. As best as I can tell, the average kid needs three cards by the end of the first year. Now that I've told you that, you don't have to get too crazy when your child loses one. But you can make your child wait for ten days while you order a replacement set from the bank. You wanted tough lessons; this is another good one.

Finally, show your child how to withdraw money from the ATM machine. This is actually quite important, as many machines "eat" a card that is not properly identified by its code. If you have anticipated this need, your child may have had the opportunity to practice using your ATM card once or twice and will already be familiar with the drill.

Recognize the power of the card. This is a very potent symbol of adulthood. Aside from a driver's license, it represents one of the most significant symbols of passage from childhood to adulthood. Getting this card is an ego boost to your child that will make him or her very proud. Do not let it pass into your child's hands without due notice and celebration.

CHAPTER FIVE

My ATM Card Is Broken

Using an ATM card is a skill. It takes clear-headed, focused attention to approach the icon of financial freedom and to maneuver one's way through all its intricacies. Don't believe me? Watch your teens. Do they ever want to get it right! They will learn each of its blunders in turn.

Blunder Number One: Messing Up the Card

They will demonstrate the "can't remember the PIN number" gambit first. This blunder is quickly corrected. No number, no money. They learn their PIN.

Blunder Number One also encompasses the many ways one can destroy, lose, inactivate, or otherwise make worthless an innocent two-inch-by-three-inch piece of magnetized plastic. It encompasses every possible way to manhandle it, mangle it, lose it, write on it, demagnetize it, give it away, leave it at McDonald's, or use it to break into a sibling's room.

Another form of Blunder Number One is to write one's PIN on the back of the card. No, no. "So why did you write it on the back of yours,

Dad?" Learning bad habits is often by example.

There are more faulty behaviors for your kids to learn. I'm giving you a recipe book of possibilities. These "recipes" detail the means by which creative, motivated, technologically savvy teens mess up their ATM cards.

If you are following the methodology of this book, this is where you and your teen start. It is the first real search for the Holy Grail of financial independence. This is also where Blunder Number Two happens.

Blunder Number Two: Spending Everything at Once

This blunder is more insidious than finding every possible way in which to manhandle the card. It is: spend everything, all at once, quickly. Teens almost inevitably make Blunder Number Two because it is the first opportunity for them to express adolescent independence. You are giving your teens money without strings, independence without experience, responsibility without judgment. They are on the edge of the cliff, eager to jump off into the mists below. They will use up every penny. (Remember the suggestion that you put just one month's worth of money at a time into the account? That lowers the height of the cliff.)

Place some limit on that spending behavior so you can maintain your sanity and your personal assets. If you followed my advice and put just a limited amount of money in their account, you will still have enough left over to pay your own shelter, heat, and food bills.

An ATM card allows you to create a small universe of independence for your teen in which it is safe to learn from making mistakes.

Many banks provide an ATM card for accounts with a small minimum balance. In Wisconsin the minimum balance that our local bank permits is $200. If your bank does the same, that $200 is yours, the adult's. The bank also automatically deducts the chosen amount from your checking account each month to be deposited into your teen's account. That money becomes your teen's.

"So, get this straight. Your account will always have two hundred bucks more in it than you get to spend. That is my money." Say this twenty times to your teens when you open up their accounts so you get it out of your system, because that money will soon belong to someone else. Your kids will spend it. That is their job. Remember, Blunder Number Two is to spend all the money you can get your hands on all at once, as soon as you get it.

Throughout history societies have invented a variety of means by which teens can make the transition to adulthood: sweat lodges, drum beating, starvation-induced hallucinations, and the like. In America in the late twentieth century we invented the driver's license and the fraternity/sorority drinking party to accomplish something on that order. A rite of passage signifies that the youth has achieved adult power. He or she now has the keys to the sanctioned transactions of adult society.

But the modern American teen operating on the Capitation Method will demonstrate the invention of a new version of initiation into the financial techno-era. Your teens will demonstrate their adult power by taking their friends to the ATM terminal and making it give them money. Magic!

Once the ATM has done its duty, the first phrase from your teen's mouth to his or her assembled friends is, "Let's all go to McDonald's, guys. My treat. Didn't your parents give you enough money? No prob. I've got plenty. Let me show you."

Standing in front of the ATM and hearing ffft, ffft, ffft, ffft, ffft as the machine counts out nice neat, crisp twenties, your teenager's friends are impressed. A hundred bucks in three seconds. That's power!

You will find reference to ATMs in the Bible. Remember the story of the Prodigal Son? He must have been a pretty nice guy. Wanted all his buddies to have a really good time at the local fast-food joint. Went to the ATM and got twenty shekels in a jiffy. Chink, chink, chink. His dad made a much worse blunder: gave him his entire inheritance all at once. Today we call this error the Uniform Gift to Minors Act. The Prodigal Son was soon dead broke and ended up feeding pigs. Probably couldn't remember where he blew all his spare change. Two thousand years later, same story.

If you want to sound cool, you can say, "Been there, done that, got the T-shirt." Watch your teens roll their eyes. It's a better line than, "That's my money." Remember, you said that twenty times and got it out of your system before you started. It's so square. You need to be "radical" to impress teens today. And were you so perfect when you were a teen?

The purpose of an ATM card at age fourteen or so is to help your children learn this lesson before the pig-feeding stage becomes much more expensive. (Now you know why college fraternities are called Animal Houses. The moneyed animals all live there.) Ffft, ffft, ffft, ffft. It is a sweet sound. And so irresistible. The sound of the American consumer who has completed his or her rite of passage, updated from the biblical chink, chink, chink. The new adult.

The image in your teen's mind as he or she stands on the threshold of the mall is no different from the image of that grand old American archetype, the western cowboy on his horse, looking out over the endless prairie that offers fame and fortune for the taking. Yippee. Ride 'em, cowboy. Enter the mall and flash your card. Ffft, ffft, ffft. There's more where that came from.

As you sit in your car and watch one of your teens at the ATM terminal pounding on the machine in frustration, close your eyes and picture the Amazon jungle. Listen to the drums beating through the forest. Watch the smoke curling up from the initiation hut. Try to smile. It beats weeping.

If each ffft equals a twenty, it will take your teens between one and two weeks to spend all of their first month's money, and all of yours.

You can wait. Play coy and innocent. Sit reading the paper. You will be approached with the following: "Dad, can you help me figure this out? I think the ATM card is broken. Can you call the bank?"

"What do you mean, it's broken?"

"Well, maybe it's just my card. I put my card in the machine, and it didn't give me any money."

Do not snicker, wave your finger, or act pompous. Remember, they are sharing their turmoil with you while they are safe at home. This could be happening to them when they are nineteen, living in a dorm two thousand miles away from home, and much deeper in the hole.

"Have you spent all your money?"

"Oh, no. I couldn't have."

"How much have you taken out?"

"We just went to the mall last weekend." (Remember, the mall is code for ffft, ffft, ffft. An ATM can count out $100 in about three seconds.)

"Have you checked your balance?"

"No, the machine ate my card."

"We have to call the bank to get it back."

"Really?"

(No, I just go to the machine and hit it and it gives it to me. I am all-powerful Nimrod, the card hunter.) "Yeah, it takes about two weeks to get another one."

"But I don't have any money and I have to go to the amusement park this week with my friends."

"Weren't amusement parks in your budget?"

"Yeah, but I can't get at my money. Can you lend me some?"

Alarm, alarm, alarm. There is another way out. Call the bank. Most have twenty-four-hour customer service reps. (You made a photocopy of the card, didn't you?) Find out the balance. The odds are fifty to one that "the card doesn't work"/"the ATM machine is broken" because the account is empty.

Yup. Every penny. Theirs and yours. There is no money.

"The ATM machine is broken" and "the card doesn't work" are classic lines. Be honest. Did the phrase "My checking account couldn't be empty, I still have checks" ever cross your lips? Different era, same mistake. Call the bank. Data speaks for itself.

"It looks as though your balance is under $10. That's why the machine wouldn't give you any money. Any idea how that happened?"

"You're kidding. I couldn't have. I only went two or three times. We just went to Mickey D's. Just a few friends . . . ."

At this point you can trot out your biblical reference to the Prodigal Son and have your teen stomp out on you. It will give you more free time this weekend. Alternatively, a sympathetic comment about how easy it is to spend all one's money in a week or two on simple things is still painful to hear but might make for a better relationship.

Blunder Number Three: Not Planning Ahead

Your teens are now coming face to face with the reality of Blunder Number Three: Not Planning Ahead. They have spent all their money, flexed all their independence, completed their rites of passage. They have toyed with the forbidden fruits of temptation and given in to the impulses of popularity, prestige, and status. How fast those false values fade away when the ATM machine is silent. And now they are broke! (Another peculiar American rite of passage.)

It is time to do a reality check. This is the most important part. You want to initiate your teens into a different kind of adulthood than they imagined. You want them to grasp the values of an adulthood that takes pride in being responsible, pride in living within one's means, and savors confidence in knowing how to solve the never-ending problems of financial limitations. Planning ahead and learning limits are skills best learned by experiencing limitations. Plant the next question ever so gently.

"How are you going to buy new school clothes next month if all your money next month goes to rebuilding the minimum?" Major reality shock wave. Near panic. Tough lesson. Silence.

"You know, I have to mow the lawn this weekend. If you were to mow it instead, I bet I could pay you for it. Let's see, minimum wage is $____ an hour for adults so I could pay you $____." They will get the point. It will happen.

Save the 126 bottles of nail polish your daughter buys the first month or your son's shoebox of baseball cards. Ten years from now they will laugh. This month, they are in the pigpen and have to find a way to get out. Pride has to fall a long way before one climbs out. In the meantime the ATM will not make its magic sound for them. Nor will they go to the Amusement park with their friends.

Reality starts to set in. Money is not unlimited. ATMs do not print money. Having an ATM card in the pocket does not mean one is rich. Life moves forward. The rest of the American rite of passage has to take place. Independence and responsibility have to go hand in hand. Responsibility and consequences are first cousins, related through experience.

For those of you whose children never go through this stage, you can stop reading this book and send them straight to the Wharton School of Business. Perhaps Harvard or MIT already has a spot for them. The rest of us have mortal children. Tread gently. Learning happens by mistake, and the first time is almost always the hardest.

Your teens will learn other variations on Blunders Number One, Two, and Three. They cannot carry an ATM card in an empty pocket without it getting bent or lost. Bent cards do not work. Demagnetized cards also do not work. Lost cards work the least. Your kids will learn they must keep track of their cards. Banks should really issue six at a time. You know: "Hey, you a teenager doing this Whitcomb capitation stuff? Let me order you a six-pack."

An ATM card cannot be used to pry open bottles, get into the room of a sibling, scrape ice off a snowboard, or anything else that deforms and injures it. Neither will it work if someone tries to scratch off the dark brown magnetic stripe on the back. There are no secret messages under the stripe. Technology is fragile and requires due respect.

But teens are also fragile and require due respect. Letting them make Blunders Number One, Two, and Three respectfully teaches them how to win the whole ballgame. But hold the line and do not give in. The connection of consequences to behavior must be made. No pain, no gain. No drums, no adulthood. Rites of passage are still rites of passage. Immutable truths.

CHAPTER SIX

STEPPING UP TO THE NEXT LEVEL:
A GLOBAL BUDGET

This chapter gets you started on turning over a full budget to your teens: a Global Budget. By making them responsible for balancing a budget that covers all their needs and wants, you are training them in some of the most important of life's lessons.

With a little luck your kids have already acquired some financial savvy. You have spent a year together on their Clothing Budgets and are still speaking to each other. Your children have survived Blunders Number One, Two, and Three and are showing progress in their learning.

Or maybe you have kids with good heads on their shoulders and you want to start at the Global Budget level. Maybe you are just impatient and want to get started quickly with a child who is twelve months away from going to college and needs to get some experience under her or his belt.

In any case the process is roughly the same. You need to involve your kids in the decision. You need to devise a method by which you agree on the right amount for a budget. You need to agree on what should be included in that Global Budget. And you should write it down. Finally, consider the options for delivering money from your account to your children's accounts.

Getting teens interested in managing their own money is not hard. I have observed that the answer is "yes" before a parent finishes any sentence ending with a question mark that contains the words "you" and "want money." But let's be serious. A fuller discussion is in order. To plan the budget, sit down at the kitchen table during your monthly review. Pry the phone out of your teen's ear and make sure that no friends are sitting in the driveway honking a car horn while you talk. This is heavy stuff.

It is good to preface your discussion with sentences such as, "I want to find a way to work with you so that you can handle your own finances without my interference," and, "I want to be fair about how we do this but still allow you to make your own decisions." How about, "You're old enough and I trust you to do a good job learning how to manage your own finances." Follow that with, "If you like this experiment, we can go further next year and try some more ideas, like helping you with a checkbook or something like that."

By this point in any discussion the phone will have rung three times from impatient friends, and you may have to limit the first conversation. Escape quickly while you have your teen's interest and conclude with, "Let's sit down and figure out how we can do this some time this week." Your teen will come back to you.

Talk about the issue. Emphasize trust, responsibility, autonomy, and just plain growing up. The progression is not so hard if you and your children have been meeting on a monthly basis over the previous year or two and they have progressed from making the Clothing Budget to being responsible for buying their own clothing with an ATM account. Going over their bank statements leads easily to saving receipts from their clothing purchases and then to saving receipts from all their other categories of needs.

Get to the nitty-gritty quickly. Teens are not good at long philosophical discussions; they are just as happy for you to put your bucks where your mouth is. What items should be on the list for which they will be responsible?

My suggestion boils down to this:

"We feed you, take you to the doctor, buy capital goods (such as sheets, light bulbs, beds, the house) and *Really Big Things* (such as vacation tickets, skis, a bike, the class trip to Washington, D.C.). *You pay for Everything That Affects Only You.*"

An example of a list you and your child might draw up together appears in the Global Budget Contract (pp. 164–166).

Best Guess Global Budget

In order to create the Global Budget, you need to engage in some creative thinking about your expectations. You might want to list some things you really want your kids to do or continue to do. "Yes, you really do have to buy a present for your sister/brother at the holidays." "How about some money to save or some money to contribute to worthy causes?"

Talking about these expectations ahead of time takes the pain out of later misconceptions. Think ahead about how you are going to help your kids carry out such abstractions. If you want them to save some money regularly or give something to charitable causes, your kids will need to have some means for generating sufficient cash to do so. You have control of the financial world you are creating for them. Is it your expectation that they will work and earn some cash? Will you drive them to the bank each month so they can deposit money in a savings account? Will you expect them to put some money in the offering plate at your place of worship? Those activities all take extra effort on your part.

The step that comes next is to decide how you come to a budget level that works. As with the Clothing Budget I can offer you three methods.

1. Just jump in and get started with some sort of amount.
2. Follow your spending for a year on all the items you want to include. (See Lesson Plan One pp. 101–108.)
3. Sit down at the table and make your "best guess" from a budget table such as this one:

BEST GUESS GLOBAL BUDGET

Clothes	$1,000
Shoes	250
Sports	300
Winter clothes	250
Haircuts	40
School supplies	120
Pocket money	240
Gifts	200
Total	**$2,400 a year, or $200 a month.**

Do you want to include savings? Contributions? Add them in.

Finally, let's put this all in a contract, just as with the clothes. It's more complicated, and a little longer. Write it out again. Sign it. Keep a copy for each of you. (See the sample Global Budget Contract, pp. 164–166, in the last section of the book. This can be downloaded as well from www.capitateyourkids.com.)

CHAPTER SEVEN

GOING TO THE PROM FOR A BUCK

"Can I go to the prom? The freshmen are invited." "Of course you can go! How can I help? Remember, I think that was included in the contract. Let's take a look. Yes, it is part of your budget." Smug self-satisfaction. We won't have to take out the second mortgage this month after all.

Proms are special events that require planning ahead—way ahead. Birth is not too early. Planning for proms is right up there with saving for college and funeral planning. It is not difficult to spend mucho dinero for clothing rental, flowers, courtesy gifts—and that is all before your kid gets to dinner. Don't forget the most dreaded item of all: "Dad, last year everyone had a limo . . . ?" A prom is enough to break the budget of any stout-hearted parent, much less a well-intentioned adolescent.

We started the first prom year shopping for shoes for my fourteen-year-old son, David. Until then virtually all shoes that made it into the Whitcomb house were sneakers. High-tops. Suddenly, they were no longer de rigueur. Considering the "in" baggy look, I found the idea that prom fashion could include high-tops actually appealing to me with a sort of civic justice. Back in the real world a trip to our local department store meant $70 for a pair of nice black leather dress shoes. Nerdy. Teen culture shock.

When David and I walked past the men's department and saw cheap suits with price tags of $190, I felt trouble brewing. The couple arguing outside the formal wear rental store made my stomach twist into high acid knots. Through the window I could see a teen being fitted for a tux, looking about as happy as our dog being put into his winter walking sweater. We avoided the rental store.

The mood was somber on the way home. When we got home with only shoes, the first comment on our prom shopping foray was, "You made me buy that pair! I didn't even like them."

In my mind I was thinking, rent or buy a tuxedo, take a second mortgage, or move to Sri Lanka? It's always warm there. With this as a start how were we to tackle the pants, shirt, jacket? We were already almost halfway through his whole monthly budget, and all we had were shoes, which he needed anyway. The annual average income in Sri Lanka is less than the cost of this prom. I could live there and feel rich. I began to feel discouraged.

Ol' Frugal-Hand Grandpa was not so easily deterred. Nothing like experiencing fifteen years of the Great Depression to create an attitude in sharp contrast with a millennium teen.

"How about we drop by the thrift shop."

Thrift shop!!! Are you kidding? A teenager from the 'burbs in a thrift shop!

Well, why not? Under cover of darkness, using back entrances and disguises and two large adults, it is possible to drag a teen into a thrift store. (Remember to check all license plates in the parking lot first to ensure there are no familiar faces inside.) Twenty minutes later we had bought a nice midnight blue wool suit for a dollar. One buck. Nice fit. I volunteered to pay for the dry cleaning. Add a white shirt, a corsage, and we were set.

Total cost for the prom: $71. Since David needed the shoes anyway to escape sneakerdom, the real cost over base line was one dollar.

Imagine driving two fourteen-year-old couples to the prom, and the discussion between the girls, all crinkly chiffon and flashing braces, is solely about their dresses. The boys, with slicked-back hair and neat dark suits, aren't saying a word. Nor am I. For the power-deficient parent in need of future data to use in the eternal war against adolescent genius, think of the deep debt created by your teen's not having to answer the question, "Hey, nice suit, where'd you get it?" The smile on my face as I drove four kids to their Denny's Restaurant dinner in my six-year-old, paid-for Voyager "limo" was hidden in the autumn dusk.

What's the lesson here? The same blue wool suit has worked for five or six more pretty formal occasions. Had we really planned the full price of that suit or the prom into the budget? Maybe not, and maybe giving a little is okay when you get to such a crisis—so split the cost if it feels outrageous. Not every thrift shop has a suit or a dress that will work.

But thrift shops do have wonderful bargains on some things you may not be in need of immediately but that fill another need. While we were at the thrift store looking for the suit, we also found a wonderful sheepherder's winter coat for one dollar and bought that, too.

Planning ahead for big costs doesn't happen the first time. Messing up the first time helps your teen learn to plan ahead. Until you have felt the weight of large, unexpected costs coming down on you, saving up for those occasions is not a natural priority. Planning ahead for a prom is no different from planning ahead for a wedding, a car, a house, a college education. The main thing that separates proms from those other expenses encountered later is the passion of teenage hormones overlaid on unexpectedly high expense.

I now know, several safe years later, that the adolescent involved was quite proud of our frugal transaction. Almost as proud as I was of him. Would this have been true if the money saved had been mine instead of his?

CHAPTER EIGHT

LUNCH MONEY

"It's pizza day today. Can I have five dollars for lunch?" Does that question ever resound off the walls of your kitchen at breakfast? The timing is usually thirty-five seconds before the school bus is due to arrive, which, if they miss it, results in your driving them to school. Coming at that point in the morning, the question also distracts you from asking such questions as, "Did you make your bed?" or "Why didn't you pack your lunch?" You have ten seconds to produce the wallet and the cash because it takes fifteen seconds to walk down the driveway, and if the bus has pulled out, even an Olympic sprinter couldn't catch this bus driver.

It struck me how much school lunch costs when one of my friends told me she gives her son five dollars every day for school lunch and $20 every weekend for the food he has away from home. That's $170 a month in food money!

Sorry, Charlie, not in the "It's-your-money" household! Sure, I spring for an occasional treat. But let's make it a treat, not the norm. Pizza once a week isn't a treat, it's routine. A treat should be for some job well done—and maybe less often than once a week.

How about this: "We will buy you whatever lunch ingredients you wish that are not prepackaged. You pack your lunch every day. Tell us the lunch ingredients and bread type you like, the fruit you want, the cookies you like, and the potato chips you can put in a Baggie, and we'll make sure the cupboard is always stocked. Free. You want to buy pizza every week, go right ahead. We think that part of your budget is there for special treats. Think about when you want to spend your money on pizza and plan for it. We always have lunch meat, fruit, cheese, peanut butter, and cookies at home."

Free. Nice concept.

Guess who makes my kids' lunches every night around about 10 P.M.? It's a scene we don't witness. Parents of teens are usually unconscious by 9:30 P.M. But I see the bags in the fridge in the morning and the mayo smears on the counter when I get up. I beam with pride at their self-sufficiency as I mutter under my breath and clean up the counter.

Grocery bill for lunch supplies for two teens for a month: about $40. You do the math.

What are you accomplishing with this approach? You are imprinting a Fiscal Fable about frugality at precisely the time your kids can see its relevance. If they are not frugal with their lunch money, how will they ever develop the inner resources of emotional resolve to be frugal in other matters? If they cannot make the connection between spending vital resources on junk food and not having enough money for clothes at age fourteen, how will they make the same connection at age twenty-five, or thirty-two, when they need to buy a car or a house?

The imprinting of attitudes has to start at the age at which first contact is made with the relevant choices. A need for lunch money provides a pivotal opportunity to highlight the choices and consequences between frugality and wastefulness. A lesson that will last a lifetime comes from making the connection through a daily habit in which a few cents here and a dollar there add up to a significant sum. The increments seem so small in each instance that it appears justified to give in once. But you understand the connection between giving in once and making a habit. Your kids do not. They need to learn that lesson at the point of first exposure.

It is such an important lesson, it may even help for you to do the math with them. Add up the pennies it costs to make a lunch at home versus buying one at school. Multiply that by five days a week and four weeks a month. Calculate the cost of one can of Coke in a twelve-pack bought at a gasoline station's promotion. Compare that cost to twelve cans purchased from a vending machine. Make a big deal about the difference. Your emotional reaction is something your kids will internalize.

Imprinting. Fiscal Fabling. Your values. Your job.

CHAPTER NINE

WILL YOU CUT MY HAIR, DAD?

How many times have you spent Saturday morning at the local haircut joint, waiting for your kid's turn, reading stale *People* magazines? Then your kid's name is called by "the lady nobody, like nobody, can stand." This is announced at the checkout counter as "that lady" is ringing up your charge, necessitating your adding a five-dollar tip just to pay off the insult. The hope is that the next time she cuts your child's hair, she won't let the razor slip right over his carotid artery. Instead, with some polite effort on your part, she will leave that pleasure to you.

As you are being conciliatory and easy with the cash, a two-ounce bottle of Paul Mitchell hair goo shows up on the counter. "It's been marked down, see? It was $19.95 and now it's only $17.00!" A well-timed glower from behind the counter leads you to the suspicion that these two are in cahoots against you. They have really spent those twenty sweaty minutes together conspiring on how best to dismantle your financial inhibitions. The killer blow comes with, "Dad, everything we have at home makes my hair look like I'm a geek. All I get are knots, and the shampoo makes my hair green—same color as the bottle. I really need this stuff."

Remind me next time I go to the barber's to stop at the bank first with my wheelbarrow.

"Good idea, Dad. You know, I really like Studio 780. They have really nice stylists there. This lady does a hatchet job. I refuse to let her cut my hair ever again. I can't be seen in public with this mess for at least two weeks."

Let me guess—the basic haircut at Studio 780 is $22, and the goop off their shelf is never marked down. Having to be out of sight for two weeks—well, don't tempt me.

Add $10 a month to the budget for haircuts, toiletries, grooming products, and sundry goops and greases, and you never have to be the object of teen extortion again. You know the drill. Say, "I will buy basic soap, basic shampoo, basic toothpaste, and toilet paper. The bathroom supply shelf will be stocked with these basics for your free use. Anything else, it's your budget. If you want to go to Studio 780, I will drive you."

Free is one of those little four-letter jobbies. Funny psychology—"free" sort of works on you. The next step is to realize that with a sheet, some nice scissors, a misting squirt bottle, and a stool, you, too, can become a pretty accomplished hair cutter. Free.

"I will cut your hair for free," you say. "I can do it in thirty minutes, no lines, no old magazines, no hideously expensive, tempting hair goop, my time, my kitchen, Wheel of Fortune on the tube." And free.

We've been doing this for a year now, at the request of my teens. With cautious progress, I am even feeling better about doing it. And my kids have actually said, "Good job, Dad." Once.

In the supply closet is a steady stock of Ivory soap and Pert shampoo. We consent to any other shampoo that costs the same price per ounce. There are no recent arrivals in the goop category.

This Christmas I asked Santa for a real barber's sheet and a nice pair of scissors. Santa found these items at a local hair salon supply house.

My kids learned all about free, and if the truth be known, I like the time I get with my kids. Free! It's a good Fiscal Fable.

The principle here? Do it yourself! Lots of services can be purchased for a fee. With a little resourcefulness, those same services can be done at home.

Being Resourceful and Solving Problems for Yourself Is Important

This is another significant imprinting opportunity. Creating the habit of taking care of your service needs at home is directly in contrast to the world of peer-conscious teens who want desperately to fit in with prevailing fashion. Prevailing fashion usually requires an increment of skill not possessed at home. If not available at home, it must be paid for. Services that are paid for constitute a choice for the allocation of resources that are then not available for other choices.

If you can teach your teens to feel okay about resisting the temptations of peer pressure for fashion, you have started on the way to resisting living by fashion. If he or she can resist having the latest haircut at the fanciest salon, he or she can also resist having to purchase clothes at the trendy boutique. Feeling good about those victories at age fifteen creates the groundwork for feeling good about more expensive choices later in life: choosing between a new Porsche Boxster and a used Ford Escort.

True happiness does not come from owning a Porsche Boxster. True happiness starts with having the emotional maturity to be able to choose values other than the frantic rush after material possessions that you cannot afford. Learning resourcefulness around providing your own services is part of creating the emotional maturity to be content with what possessions you have. Once you are skilled at living within your means, you are off the treadmill of materialistic envy.

CHAPTER TEN

THE REAL COST OF A TRIP TO WALGREENS

I bet you think a trip to a Walgreens Drug Store is a quick little errand to get some toothpaste. That may be true in your current state of fiscal relationships. In the world of Capitated Kids, Walgreens is war. For many reasons, just "Don't go there."

It's really like this.

The rules are: "I buy basic commodities like soap, toothpaste, and shampoo. No, I do not buy salon shampoos. If you want those, that is your money."

The contract you and your teen sign should explain that the parent purchases prescription drugs. If a doctor writes a prescription, it is part of the agreed-upon responsibilities of the parent. Health insurance may even pay for it.

Then comes Walgreens, or Osco, or any another pharmacy superstore. The No-Man's-Land. Full Money Jacket. Land mines not yet banned from the face of this earth. It is the zonal boundary where rules are defined. It is where "It's your money" meets "It's my money."

Explain to me the boundary between Retin-A, the prescription written for the acne of a teen with one tiny pimple, and the huge variety of snake oils sitting on a six-foot-long shelf offering various concentrations of benzoyl peroxide and other sure-cure remedies. You may not be able to define the boundary, but your teens can. Into the red plastic shopping basket slips a bottle of Zit-Zapper-Plus, then two, and then, when you aren't watching, a six-year supply, just in case you aren't feeling so generous the next time.

You agree to buy school supplies. Does that mean you are willing to buy a new two-inch, three-ring binder, a twelve-pack of ballpoint pens, three huge sheets of poster board, a set of colored magic markers, a pencil box, a glue stick, a spiral notebook, and a new pack of mechanical pencils with leads for a school report due next Friday?

"I thought we bought all your school supplies at the beginning of the year," you mutter vacantly as the shopper behind you, who owns two hundred shares of Walgreens stock, rubs her greedy little hands together and watches the cash register paper cascade onto the floor. No one, you think, could use so many supplies unless they were running something covert. In the back of your mind you consider visiting the school in disguise to purchase back all your supplies from the black market store your teens are running out of their lockers.

You can see it now—the school newspaper's lead article headlined "LockerGate Notebook Caper Uncovered: Black Market in Excess School Supplies Found in Locker of Teen on 'Global Budget.'" Crisis in the Whitcomb house. Hostages taken. Independent prosecutor sought. You snap back into consciousness. It's the checkout counter at Walgreens, not the evening news. You have been defeated. Your teens run better covert operations than you do.

It happened at Walgreens, of all places. Just when you felt it was safe to venture forth shopping again as a family. "Let's have a nice family outing to the store," you said to yourself as you left the house. You went only to get toothpaste. How could you end up with a bill for $93.34 when all you wanted was clean teeth?

The drug/personal toiletries store is the kind of place where all the boundaries meet—or crash—between what you are willing to purchase with your money and what your teens are determined to extract out of your hide. Ambiguity is hell. Undefined boundaries are breeding grounds for conflict.

When you left the house, you did not bring the contract with you. You did not anticipate that you had to define whether or not you would pay for combs. Will you pay for one of those little brushes that clean under the fingernails? If so, write it down. If not, write it down. Does shampoo mean you pay for conditioner? Do you buy more than a twelve-year supply at one time? Do you require proof that the last bottle is finished? Do you spring for floss? Are hair bands included? Will you pay for color or tint?

"I put it in when I wash my hair!"

How about deodorant? Paying for that may be self-protection, but it opens up another whole aisle. If you pay for soap, do you pay for shaving equipment? Shaving creams, gels, powders, spritzers, scents, and razors? You get the picture.

My advice, for what it is worth now that I am crippled from tripping on all the hazards myself, is to think deeply upon these things. Then, when you drive past Walgreens and you see small groups of middle-aged parents sitting in their cars, or huddled in support groups out in the parking lot, you know they have read this book and their teens are "in there," a place where parents fear to tread. Offer to bring out a box of tissue for the huddled crowd. They will be so grateful.

The solution to shopping in undefined territory is to let your teen go in the store while you stay in the parking lot. You will be joined by another adult. Trust me.

Whosoever is not present cannot be extorted.

Either that, or take a trip to your local drugstore, inventory every item in the store, and use a highlighter to list in your teen's budget every item you will pay for. The two-and-a-half months it will take you to do this is easier work than agonizing at the checkout counter. Trust me. Been there, done that.

CHAPTER ELEVEN

WHAT DO I NEED A CHECKBOOK FOR?

An ATM card gives your teens money when they ask politely and budget appropriately. As long as your fiscally savvy, capitated teens live within their means, life is predictable. After about two years of practice your teens will be comfortable with and pretty good at planning their budgets. But if you want your teens to keep learning, you cannot stop when you get to a steady state with an ATM card.

That means it's time to expand your teens' financial horizons. One cannot accomplish all of life's financial transactions with only an ATM card. In this era checkbooks are still pretty handy, although they may become outmoded in the coming years. For now, though, many people use a checkbook to pay for a majority of their expenses. Financial institutions are just beginning to set up computerized banking from home, so paying for many standardized charges by phone and modem is now possible. Our family pays all its utility, mortgage, phone, and other monthly bills using a computer service. Still, we write twenty to thirty checks a month. So bag the argument that we are in a new age when all we need is a two-inch-by-three-inch piece of magnetized plastic to be financially self-sufficient.

"I think we should get you a checkbook. You're in eleventh grade now and have a driver's license. That means you have a picture ID and you can write checks."

"What do I need a checkbook for? Don't be a nerd, Dad. We are in the new age when all I need is a two-inch-by-three-inch piece of magnetized plastic to be financially self-sufficient."

Didn't I warn you this was coming?

Once one has lived in the world of the familiar, starting something new is always a bit disconcerting.

"No, dear, you cannot pay for everything with cash or plastic. Besides, I've always done it this way, and I don't know how you are going to pay the vendor at the craft show with a magnetized piece of plastic. She wants cash or a check."

"But Dad, I've never been to a craft show and I don't buy anything that I can't pay cash for."

Give your teen one point for tactics. This is a blunder on your part. Do not use craft show as an example. Much too middle-aged. Consider something your teens are more familiar with, like a tattoo parlor or body piercing "facility"—if you don't choke on the words.

You reply, "But it doesn't look cool to pay cash for your yearbook. You need to pay with a check so you have a receipt." Thrust and parry—this is better. You have them with the receipt ploy. Quick, while they are stuttering and hemming and hawing, throw in some reassurance and raise the ante.

"I would like to work on another project with you that gives you more money." (This particular combination of words always works.) Watch the ears perk up, the hands steady, the gaze turn to make eye contact to see if you are bluffing. This is high-stakes poker. Do not blink.

"Yes, I think we need to find a way so you have more control in your life. I would like to put your car insurance into your account and have you pay it twice a year." Quick, that's only two checks a year. You need more. "And I would like to have you pay for your music lessons out of your account, too." Really good! You're on a roll. You have their attention, but you still have to make it real. This is, after all, something you were doing for them all along. Why should they do all the work?

"But Dad, you already do all that stuff. Why should I do all the work?"

"Well, I think this is the first step." You've got to get down to real business and make it sincere. So hold on to your wallet, give up your need to control, and out with it.

"I think we should start with your paying for some simple stuff, and then next year we should add in all the rest of your expenses so that you are functioning as a grown-up without any help from me."

If you are a fisherman, you know what it is like to catch a twelve-pound Great Lakes salmon on a two-pound test line with a Number One hook. Your teens weigh considerably more, so go easy. But you do have their interest here, so reel in nice and slow. This is progress. Resistance is really happening only because it is something new.

"Sure," you go on, "I think this year you should go with easy stuff like a few checks here and there, and next year I would like you to get in the habit of running your whole show. I want to raise the ante next year so you know what it is like to live on your own. I will give you an extra $700 a month in the automatic payment, or something like that, and then you pay me for room and board with a check, just as if you were in college." (Do not mention at this point that should their behavior of coming home at 2:30 A.M. continue, you may raise their rent to $6,792 a month.)

"Okay, I guess we can do that."

"Great. Actually, I stopped by the bank last week and the teller said we could come by anytime and she would help set it up. It's pretty easy. They will show you all the kinds of accounts they have, and you get a better ATM card. It works like a credit card but takes the money right out of your checking account." That is the pièce de résistance. See, you aren't so square. You're getting your teen a debit card. That's a little accommodation to the new-age reality of needing only a little piece of magnetized plastic.

The reason to move to this level is that teens do need more than cash to function in today's complex society. Building on the complexity of ATM and budget behavior, which your teens should have in hand by now, a checkbook is a nice, concrete step that moves the budgeting process up a notch. You have to make it relevant and useful. Transferring your control over paying the usual types of bills is no skin off your nose. It is neither a net gain nor loss. Costs such as a car payment, insurance, music lessons, and school supplies, or tuition for those in parochial or private schools, are all good monthly behaviors that give your teens practice and make them familiar with paying larger bills and managing more money. A checkbook encourages documentation of expenses

There is a vital principle your teens need to learn here. In the real world over 90 percent of anyone's monthly budget does not "belong" to that person. It "belongs" to the budget categories covering food, rent, clothing, utilities, telephone, car payments, insurance, doctor's bills, savings, travel over the holidays, and summer vacation. You get the point. What little pittance is left over we call discretionary spending.

The early part of this budgeting process with your teens involved money that had some discretionary qualities to its use. One can put off buying new tennis shoes for a month. One can get along without a haircut. (This is a teen specialty.) But the new categories of financial responsibility you are proposing are nonnegotiable. Rent has to be paid. On time. Nonpayment of utility bills has the measurable consequences of darkness and cold. But just as nonnegotiable are planning and saving for larger abstract expenses such as health insurance and savings.

It is a crucial developmental step for your teens to have larger amounts of money within their realm of responsibility and control, of which only a relatively small fraction is actually available for discretionary spending.

This concept is not totally new to your teens. Their ATM accounts probably have a base amount the bank makes you put in to qualify for a free account, say $200. You hope your teens have gotten in the habit of seeing the $200 in their accounts each month as something they are not to touch. If your teens are to get their own checking accounts—which are free, allow them to write ten checks a month, and have debit card privileges—you probably need to deposit more. You will likely have to raise the minimum balance to $500 to get the level of service you desire. Again, that is "your money," not your teens'. If they have been working with ATM cards for a year or more, they are used to seeing that base amount and canceling it out of their thinking.

Adding a monthly increment to your teens' regular deposits so they can pay for their own car insurance can add a lot more. A monthly set-aside for car insurance has to accumulate over six months until it reaches the point of covering the semiannual insurance premium. Auto insurance for adolescent boys can easily cost $1,500 a year—that is, with good grades and no tickets. Bad grades and an accident can double the premium. If your teens want to drive, or you need them to drive, divide your annual insurance cost by twelve and add the sum to their monthly subsidies.

You cannot drop the ball at this point. Watch their checking accounts with them. All those new categories added at once can be a little bit of a temptation to spend more. A wonderful opportunity to do some "family bonding" on a monthly basis is to balance the checkbook together. On the premise that this should not require a therapist, two NFL referees, a CPA, and a bouncer to keep everyone on an even keel, I advise you to review your teenagers' bank statements alone before you sit down together.

Start from scratch and show your teens how to balance their checking accounts with the first two checks you helped them write and the five ATM withdrawals and two debit card purchases they made on their own. Help your teens calculate how much the balance needs to grow to be on track for the insurance premium.

Once you have gone over the process three or four times and passed one large insurance payout, your teens might beg out of your monthly bonding session. Do not be hurt; they might be learning more quickly than you think. Or they might be using all the money in the account to buy a new stereo sound system for their car and do not want you to discover the "small loan" they are making to themselves from the insurance account. In this case you may want to have your state statutes on embezzlement handy when you sit down to discuss this.

Look at it this way: your teens can try this gambit with a little bit of your money in eleventh grade and learn that they get caught, or they can try it with $10,000 on their first job and end up doing time. Your choice.

What you thought was tuition money, they will see as barely getting by. They are more likely to use up ten grand in college on little expenses here and there, not realizing that the big sums they are being expected to handle have to cover a lot more items in their budgets. The real cost of living in the lifestyle to which they have been accustomed may come as a big shock. If your teens are not educated by working through the issues earlier in their experience, it may be a shock they cannot easily handle.

The real lesson for the vast majority of our kids is quite simple and straightforward. They need the developmental task of learning judgment over larger and larger responsibilities.

Judgment is learned only by making mistakes in an environment that has the referee biased in their favor, so they learn and grow and feel proud of their good sense.

It takes time and multiple experiences to cement that judgment.

That's why your teenager needs a checkbook.

CHAPTER TWELVE

Is There Any Extra Work Around Here?

Let's say your teens are about three months into this budget thing and they are broke. Rock bottom. You can tell because they get this dreamy look in their eyes as they sit over their third bowl of breakfast cereal. They are thinking they have to bulk up at breakfast because there is no moola to buy lunch out of the junk food machines at the school cafeteria. You know, the all-American school cafeteria lunch: a bag of potato chips, a can of real sugar soda, and a candy bar, two dollars. That's what they have lived on for the last three months. And now the money is gone. But they're not quite broke enough yet to be frugal, as their grandparents would define frugal. No, no, they are not about to cut consumption just yet.

If no income is coming from the bank, how about another source? Anticipating this, you have let the grass go a few extra days. The garden hasn't been weeded. The car needs an oil change. The vacuuming hasn't been done yet this week. Let's see if they will nibble.

"I'm broke, Dad."

"Oh?"

"I really need some money for this weekend."

"What's up this weekend?"

"Well, there's this party at Justin's, and I want to get a CD to take."

"Have you got enough clothes yet?"

"Oh, yeah, didn't I tell you? Justin told me that if I brought that CD, he would give me the sweatshirt his brother gave him. And that way I don't need a sweater, and anyway a CD costs a lot less." Don't comment on these economics. Just go for the opportunity.

"Would you like to earn a little around here?"

"Sure!"

Measure the eagerness in the tone of voice. Probably you will note a certain willingness to bend to the laws of supply and demand. You call it work. This may be new.

"Well, the lawn needs cutting."

"But I don't know how to start the rider."

"I can help you start it." This is not reluctance, it is new and unfamiliar. Be encouraging. "I can think of some other chores."

"No, that's okay. I think I would like to do the lawn."

Suddenly, your teen is doing the lawn every week. In a couple of months your teen even takes pride in getting the job done smoothly and neatly.

So be creative. Think of the jobs you are not crazy about—the weekly household cleaning, cooking supper every night, changing the sheets, and doing laundry. One family we've shared this method with has their child shopping for groceries. Another babysits siblings. Each chore can have a value attached to it. Kids in their early teens are not employable because of their age. Moreover, you may not be eager to have them working outside the home when schoolwork should be a priority. Most of all, you could use the help at home on something you might already be paying for. If you eat out at fast-food places a lot, a home-cooked meal can be a lot cheaper, and the money you save can go to your kids instead of to Fast-Food, Inc. Generate your own new Fiscal Fables.

Working around the home on real jobs is a great way for a teenager to be introduced to the idea of a job outside the home. Once a teen becomes legally employable, a job outside the home is a great way to reinforce the value of labor and money.

Working six or seven hours to earn a shirt or blouse starts having a measurable impact on the way items of clothing are cared for. Can you imagine your teens ironing all their clothes? Think how you would feel if you came down to the family room to find twenty shirts on clothes hangers, all neatly ironed. Close your eyes and picture your offspring sewing a piece of black cloth over a hole in a black tennis shoe so it will last through the summer. When you ask why, you will be told it is so new shoes can be bought when school starts.

Doing jobs around the house is preparation for doing jobs outside the house. And with a budget in which your teens are globally responsible, the connection between work and reward is very definite. Once they get a sense of this, the cents will follow. This is a crucial developmental step. Observe it. Name it to yourself. Your teens might not tolerate your celebrating it overtly, but your pride is well placed.

This is the beginning of "frugal behavior." It's the idea that labor has value and can result in tangible goods. It's valuable for your kids to learn this idea by doing.

Once your teens start down this path, they begin to realize that they can perform only a certain total amount of work. The next step in that logic chain is for them to recognize that they can work less if they consume less.

The concept that limited funds can be expanded by increased work is an important one, along with the idea that they can work less if they consume less.

CHAPTER THIRTEEN

BE KIND

How hard-hearted do you have to be to achieve results? That is the $64 question. It is a good question and goes right to the core of what you are doing with this program. Consider: You send your kids to school to learn to solve problems. Hard problems. You are very proud of them when they get an A in chemistry. They are very proud when they get an A in chemistry. That A came only with a lot of hard work on tough problems. Can you apply that same analogy to the money front?

If you are not firm on most of the program, you give away the opportunity for your kids to solve the natural problems that come their way. Catch yourself when you see a problem arise, and reframe your reference point. You do not want to shield your teens from problems. You are doing this whole deal so they learn to solve their own problems. Problems are not bad, they are good. Tell yourself repeatedly that you are glad, glad, glad your teens are getting to face many problems when you are just around the corner to help if things get out of control. Better now with $100 than in five years with $5,000. In the meantime stay out of the way. Do not interfere. Let me repeat: Keep your mitts off!

What you need are tactics to prevent your natural parental instinct to rescue from taking over. When your teens come to you with long faces asking for funds, and you know they have been imprudent, refer to the contract you signed together. Most such circumstances are quickly solved as your teens rediscover just what they agreed to. At this point you will be grateful that you had the integrity to do a fair and conscientious job of figuring out how much your family spends on clothing, recreation, and all the other items in the budget. If you accomplish that process fairly, you are on safe and stable ground against your own tendency to doubt your right to be tough.

So when do you give in a little? When do you help them without undermining the basic lessons you set out to accomplish? From the families I have worked with, I have heard a variety of circumstances in which they confess to "giving in." I categorize these circumstances as the covert and the overt.

The Covert Helping Hand

You say to your teen, "Hey, I was just cleaning out the closet and found sweaters I haven't worn for a couple of years and thought I should get rid of this one. Would you like it, or should I take it to the thrift store?"

Or you are on a business trip and stay at a motel right next to a mall. How about a gift of a nice blouse or T-shirt?

Other covert opportunities include making sure extended family members know about clothing tastes at birthday times and holiday gift-giving occasions. Can you inflate the pay for doing the chores you have around the house? Are you a good solicitor for neighborhood jobs such as babysitting?

The net effect of these covert kindnesses is that you are making sure your teens are getting what they need without damaging their pride about whether their money method is working or not working. Remember, you really are crazy about these emerging human beings, and you want them to succeed and to be safe and cared for. So pick up the pieces with care and subtlety. Their pride in their success is very real.

The Overt Acts of Kindness

These are more obvious. Overt kindnesses shouldn't undermine the discipline of the methodology either. Here are some ideas for how you can help out. When you go on a family vacation, can you give them a fixed sum for "mad money" while on the trip? How about offering them gifts of money on holiday gift occasions? Can you let go every now and then for school lunch when it's pizza day at school? Can you create some extra incentives around schoolwork?

How about, "I would like to start a reward system. How about $____ in cash every time you make honor roll? I want you to work at school, and I know that jobs are hard to do when you study so hard." This offer will likely not be declined.

Kindness. It's good.

CHAPTER FOURTEEN

CHARITY, SAVINGS, IRAs, AND COLLEGE

L earning to save or to give charitably is something the perfect child should naturally know how to do. Unfortunately, the reality is that learning these behaviors takes time and develops only through practice, just like any other learned behavior. If we parents had started out as perfect children, we would be saving a lot more than we are now. Clearly, we haven't learned it well ourselves.

In the public arena in which our children function, many types of savings behaviors can be seen. If we look closely, we see that these are groups saving for specified group goals rather than individuals saving for a personal goal.

Selling chocolate-covered cherries after long church services to hypoglycemic churchgoers is one of my favorites. Who can resist chocolate from irrepressibly cheerful teens at church? And all for the good cause of funding a church trip, to boot. Car washes to raise money for school bands, Girl Scout cookies, youth group Christmas wreaths, endless pizza sales—all are methods of saving for group goals. These are efforts we see publicly. We need to look internally for what we are saving for ourselves and how we teach our kids to save for themselves.

Like the other main theme in this book of learning prudent spending habits, developing habits of saving and giving requires opportunities for learning and rewards for doing. You have to encourage savings, watch them grow, and talk about your long-term goals. Saving behavior won't start out of the blue at age thirteen, just as it doesn't start at age twenty-three. Musicians do not spring forth as maestros without having practiced. What is the savings equivalent of violin lessons?

I like fostering the saving habit from an early age. Whenever you begin to give your kids pocket money, I believe a certain amount should go into an envelope for savings and a certain amount for charity. If one doesn't walk the walk at age six, it is much harder to start at age twelve. When the child is six years old, parents have to be completely in charge. You put the money in the envelopes, and you keep the envelopes in your possession. Take the envelopes out each week, hand the pocket money out to eager little fingers, and visibly place the designated portion into the savings and charitable-giving envelope.

Just as you reward the giving of pocket money by creating circumstances in which your young child can spend it, create rewarding circumstances for saving and giving. Accumulating the savings for a big purchase makes the act of saving feel good. Encouragement, praise, and positive feedback from other adults make charitable giving feel good to your child.

One family reported encouraging saving habits by contributing a matching amount for any money their child saved from ages six through twelve. Their argument was that a six percent return on a savings account in the bank is not enough to reward children who have a reference timeline of a week.

One caution: An offer to double any money saved has a giant loophole in it. Do the math in your head. Think. Your children will figure it out if you don't. If a child puts $20 of holiday gift money into savings and you add another $20, the savings account has a new sum of $40 in it. Now your child asks to withdraw $20 from "last year's money" for a "special purpose" he or she was saving for. That money, they claim, is "old money" that was in the account before. Net effect for the kid, no loss—he or she still has $20 in hand. You just put $20 into a savings account without any effort on your kid's part. Big loss to you. If you let this happen, your children will be managing foreign currency hedge funds in their future. Very clever. If they are that good, it's time to get a real job. Wall Street, here are their résumés.

Once you start your teens on their own Global Budgets in eighth or ninth grade, you can build into your budget calculations a sum of money that you believe your children should save and a sum that you believe should be given to charity. These sums should be included in your contract so that they are mutually agreed upon ahead of time. Your teens also need to be followed up on and encouraged. The object of saving should be tangible and the end not too far into the future.

A good goal to save for could have something to do with cars. Teens have such hopes and dreams built up about cars that creating a savings goal to help in achieving that dream is very motivating and relevant. How about the premium for their insurance? Strike the bargain early.

"If you can save enough to pay for the first year's insurance, we can keep the old car I had intended to trade in and let you drive it instead." From age fourteen on you will have a savings fanatic.

If your family attends some form of worship regularly, your teens need to see you participating in charitable giving there as well as with other causes. Do not be shy in sharing your reasons for doing so. Giving regularly, with congratulations and encouragement each time you see your teens doing the same, builds a "positive balance" of good feelings about the action.

You can probably recall phrases from your childhood such as, "To whom much is given, much is expected" or "The first 10 percent goes to God, the next 10 percent to savings, and the rest to taxes." Those phrases may not work for you, but I find that children repeatedly ask you why you do what you do, and simple sentences work: "The only way to make the world a better place is for each of us to step up to the plate to do his or her part."

Once you start your teens on their Global Budgets, you have less control of their money actions. If you have written some expected behaviors into their contracts, you can call them on their compliance. If you expect them to put aside five dollars a week, make sure you spend the time to help them put it aside.

At first you will see your teens spending all their money on priorities you would not choose. Gradually they get the hang of keeping track of all their expenses. They start being more frugal and more in control of impulsive spending behavior. When they acquire that discipline, they acquire the skills necessary for thinking about saving for its own merits.

Within a year or two you will see them accumulating their money for their own priorities. Are you ready for those priorities? How about a drum set in your basement? Are you willing to see the savings being used for an M-1 target rifle for competitive shooting? A sewing machine, a bass guitar, and a car stereo system—all are examples I have heard from families who have developed similar money plans. Watch as the personalities and priorities of your teens turn into lasting hobbies. Hold your ears while they practice on their drums.

Try not to weep too openly. Remember your priorities when you were a kid. I recall a certain raw wool vest from Nepal that I wore in the seventies; it complimented my shoulder-length hair perfectly. I loved my vest. I am not sure my parents did. My wife tells me that at the time the odors emanating from that vest produced her strongest reservations about "hanging out" with me.

Long-Term Vision

Short-term saving for material objects is one thing. Those sorts of short-term goals are easily achievable. When do your teens make the transition to planning for longer-term, less material goals? Who is saving for college?

You need to be thinking about those priorities. Your teens haven't been there before and need you to be responsible for raising those sorts of issues. Some of these issues are covered in Lesson Plans One–Six which give you the step-by-step process (pp.100–159). That outlined process creates for you a rigorous method for continuously raising the level of your kids' financial thinking, all the while following the principle that they are the ones responsible for carrying it out.

As you and your teens finish planning each level of the budget, always replace that planning process with a wider vision that needs longer-term planning, longer-term budget forecasting, and longer-term savings. Keep your eye on the overarching ideas you want your kids to be absorbing from you: **Live within your means, solve problems on your own, find creative ways to avoid peer pressure about spending, perform your own services, entertain yourself without spending, save first before spending.**

Begin talking about going to college or getting some sort of advanced education or training from the day your child goes to kindergarten. Make it an expectation. State the expectation aloud that your child will save during high school for college or other training. What one works for and saves for is what one values. Buying bass guitars is not a long-term investment plan that pays meaningful rewards for the rest of life, except for the very few. College is.

Miracle of Compounding

The outline in the Lesson Plans in this book provides a method to teach the benefits of saving. Explain to your kids the miracle of compounding growth and stock market returns and risks. Talk about IRAs and Keogh pension plans—new ideas that our generation was not taught about, because those plans did not exist. Just two generations ago our elders thought they would live out their years with "nature's social security system"—their children. Our generation has made the switch to doing it on our own. Are we passing that expectation for self-sufficiency on to our children? Are we giving them the knowledge to enable them to think about it, value it, and do something about it, like saving 10 percent of their income from the day they have their first job? You must take the time to sit down and talk about these values on a monthly basis, over the years, again and again and again.

One way of teaching the miracle of compounding growth is to play a game. Have a contest in your family with a hypothetical $100,000 portfolio in the stock market. Each year award a real prize to the family member whose portfolio grows the most. Follow the stocks on a quarterly basis and map out how they do.

This type of contest requires you and your teen to sit down regularly to talk about money. The Lesson Plans (pp. 100–159) give you the format to do just that.

The plain and simple fact about learning to save is that it is not plain and simple. You have to teach it, reward it, talk about it every month, and create a graduated set of rewards that encourage it and make it concrete.

If you are really successful, will your children take care of you in your old age? Of course, because with all the loving you are showing them, they will be crazy about you. And with all the skills they learn at your loving and patient direction, they will have the resources to afford you.

CHAPTER FIFTEEN

INSURANCE:
MEDICAL, AUTO, HOME, LIFE

L earning about insurance is not in the normal curriculum for raising kids any more than learning to save is. Just where do kids
learn that medical insurance is useful stuff? How are they to
know what happens when they do not have auto insurance?

They will learn only if you talk about it, because—except for auto
insurance—there is precious little opportunity for them to need insurance products while living at home.

One way to learn to use a checkbook is to learn to account for and
save up for auto insurance. As badly as all teens want to drive, the cost
of insurance is a barrier that limits their ability to do so. Auto insurance
creates a barrier that must be taken seriously. And that becomes a moti-
vation to save seriously.

Car insurance has to be paid regularly, regardless of how your teens
drive. Make sure they are saving for it. Walk them through each step of
paying the premium. Make sure they do it on time. Make sure they read
the small print that says what happens if they do not pay it. Finally,

make sure they are the ones who pay it, not you.

Health insurance is a different affair. In case you hadn't noticed, your teens believe they have no need for health insurance. After all, they are invincible, indestructible, and immortal. We should be grateful for this belief. How would most of the great achievements in this world have been accomplished if the human race did not start out so incredibly optimistic?

I remember just after getting married being somewhat astounded when my new father-in-law went to extraordinary lengths to make sure my new bride and I had a health insurance policy—one that would cover us for only the few weeks we would be on our honeymoon until school started and school health insurance would once again cover us. Was I that reckless? What lay ahead of us that needed such concern? I didn't have a clue or a care. My bride and I were going to live forever. Never in my wildest dreams could I imagine the costs of an uninsured car accident and a lifetime in a wheelchair.

Looking back from my middle years with children of my own, I can now understand the minefields that need to be crossed for our offspring to make it safely to adulthood. But when I was their age, the thought had not crossed my mind. It couldn't have crossed my mind. We were invincible, optimistic, and immortal.

You have precious little opportunity to talk about insurance with your kids. I suggest you do one of those old-fashioned things, as the *U.S. Government Guidebook on Kids, Cash, Plastic and You* suggests: show your kids your own behavior. Show them how you fill out the deductible form for your health insurance. Let them take a look at the cost of going to the hospital and getting an X-ray of an ankle, or getting a broken arm fixed. If they do not see what the costs are, how the paper flows, and how the money flows after the paper, they will not value the need for health insurance. Each report that comes from your health insurer about where your claim is in the process of being paid becomes a valuable report to take to your monthly money talk session.

Learning this kind of stuff can be dry and tedious. If you follow the Lesson Plans (pp. 100–159), you will save every insurance receipt you get and take it to those sessions on money. This gives you real-time, relevant content for your kids to learn from. Teach them how to read the hospital billing form for the expenses incurred. And let them see the three other bills that come in from the same visit for the lab, X-ray, and other doctors that were not included in the hospital bill. Have them add it all up.

Be prepared for this to feel overwhelming to your children. They will feel guilty that you spent "so much money" on them. A broken arm can easily cost more than their entire year's budget. If you sense that feeling coming up in your conversation, you have the opportunity to inject two wonderful lessons.

Lesson Number One is, "Kids, you are worth every penny because we love you."

Lesson Number Two is, "Look at what all the costs were and how little we had to pay by ourselves because we had insurance that covered it!" That makes health insurance look like a pretty good deal. Now it has value. It pays for the unexpected catastrophe.

Knowing you are going to do this sort of teaching when medical emergencies arise gives you a positive frame of mind to maintain when emergencies actually happen. Medical emergencies are always a rude interruption of whatever you were doing. As you find yourself pulled away from your favorite Sunday afternoon football game to take your daughter to the emergency room because she can't walk, having fallen on the stairs (up which she was running pell-mell), repeat to yourself, "This is a good learning experience. I will now have the material to show her just how valuable health insurance is." Say this silently ten times. She needs sympathy as you drive to the hospital, not a tongue-lashing. Besides, the game will be on the television in the emergency room lobby.

With just a wee bit of luck, your child will never use another penny of health coverage. Use the opportunity when you get it.

How about the universe of all the other kinds of insurance out there? Same point. Have you ever had a claim on your homeowner's insurance?

Make sure your kids see the claim form and get a chance to talk about it with you. Can you save the insurance claim to fill out with them at your monthly "money talk"?

Disability, life insurance, trusts, and so on are beyond the scope of this book. I think talking about them is great. Your kids do not need them now but will not be harmed if they have the opportunity to be exposed to the ideas. If you have a trust, you can show your kids in an outline form how it works.

CHAPTER SIXTEEN

You Gotta Talk the Talk and Walk the Walk

Y

ou've got the method. Now you need to apply it in the context of your family. Money management skills are very closely aligned with many other family values, making a universal formula or set of rules impossible to formulate. What is not impossible, and in fact is crucial, is that you, the parent, make a link between those values that you hold dear and the messages you give your children. Here are some tips I believe will help you understand how to transmit those values.

I believe children inherit their parents' emotional state of mind in response to specific triggers. Let me explain. Every time you, the parent, come across a particular situation that involves your spending money (let's call it a trigger), you display a certain attitude toward that situation. Your attitude may be one of frustration because of the high price, astonishment at the good value, anger over the unexpected, or laissez-faire about the cost.

Let's assume for the purpose of an example that you display an attitude of laissez-faire. You are in an amusement park and encounter a soda machine that advertises cold soda at twice the price you usually pay. You have no other options for purchasing cold liquids. Nonchalantly you pay the dollar. Your children are watching. You have just programmed them to be nonchalant about the cost of a soda, even when it is a dollar.

Consider an alternative emotion. You register irritation about the cost of the soda. You say something like, "Holy Toledo, look how much they charge when they have you at their mercy!" No way are you going to pay that high price. Ingeniously you fish out of your backpack a water bottle of homemade lemonade. You comment to your kids how clever you are for saving the cost of the soda, as you knew the day would get hot. "See why we packed the lemonade ahead of time? Among us, we have just saved enough to pay for half a ticket for one of us." You have demonstrated to your children frugality and problem solving.

My observation about my children is that their emotional memory is all subconscious and intuitive but a virtual dead ringer for my own. I hear words from their mouths that I have never spoken, but that sound identical to the tone of voice and intent of message I might have chosen in the same circumstances. I am convinced, based on no data but my own observations, that our emotional memory is a much more basic and lasting memory, more primal and fundamental to our being than our conscious memory.

Imprinting

Can you remember where you were when the space shuttle Challenger blew up? Or when Kennedy was assassinated? Can you remember a car accident you had? Every time you drive past the place of that accident, don't you remember the same fear and anger you first felt? Those are all examples of traumatic emotional memories replaying themselves. You were emotionally imprinted by the accident. Although I'm using dramatic examples with traumatic emotions, it nonetheless demonstrates the point.

Have you ever observed the fear that animals who have been hunted exhibit when you come into their presence? Have you noted how their offspring immediately copy their parent's fleeing behavior as humans approach? Observe those same species in Yellowstone National Park where they have not been harmed by humans for many generations. Fear is absent. To the best of our knowledge animals do not pass on intellectual memory. However, it is easy to observe them training their offspring with their emotional memory—a memory that affects behavior profoundly and fades slowly over many generations.

Humans have many of the same instinctual emotional responses to certain situations. Yet we are different from animals in our ability to talk about our thoughts and emotions, thereby making our imprinting process more complex. We are heavily dependent on our parents for years of sheltering and training while we mature. At the same time I believe we imprint from our parents' complex emotional responses in much the same fashion as the rest of the animal kingdom.

How do we imprint? Our parents expose us to the world around us and offer us their cultural attitudes toward that world. We listen to their stories, we observe their emotions, and we watch their behavior.

Here is the rub. With such rapid change in the world, the cultural attitudes we inherit from our predecessors are not in synchrony with the modern world of sophisticated economic transactions. Our kids need to be financial gurus, and we, their parents, are still dealing with unarticulated feelings inherited from our own parents who grew up in the Great Depression. We have not yet developed a financial terminology—a fiscal folklore, if you will—for how to cope with credit card debt or retirements that last for forty years. Today our fiscal responses still demonstrate attitudes from the Depression era.

How do the children of the Depression—our parents and grandparents —think of teenagers in the current era? With dismay at seeing teens walk out of a room leaving "all the lights on." Confused by their grandchildren putting little value on savings or the frugal behaviors of the thirties, the conversations of elders often demonstrate great distress over the attitudes of their grandchildren toward money.

The culture of frugality is the emotional memory that the current generation of parents inherited and is unconsciously trying to pass on to their teens. Does it work? Not always. Can we make a change? Of course, if we know where our feelings come from and recognize the messages we are putting out there for our children to absorb.

To successfully influence our children in their attitudes about money, I believe we need to talk the talk and walk the walk. That is, we need to display through our own words and behaviors the values we want our children to inherit. We need to create new myths and stories to enculturate our children in the current era of financial responsibility. Such stories must be communicated in the vital context in which the relevant situation occurs. I'm not talking sweat lodge myths and epic tales; I'm talking shopping mall myths and Fiscal Fables.

Be alert for opportunities to talk about the values you want to pass on and to demonstrate through your own actions the skills of money management. You want your children to have money management skills. You want them to be able to articulate a budget and to live within that budget. You want them to know how to plan ahead and save up for important items. You want them to know how to keep track of money in its various means of dispersal: a checkbook, an ATM card, a credit card.

In addition, you want them to have some money values—to spend resources based on utility more than peer pressure. You want them to value abstract goals—to recognize that getting a college education has greater value than getting a stereo system. You want them to be able to delay gratification—not forever, but long enough to accomplish important goals. You want them to learn how to accumulate wealth and be happy with the lifestyle in which wealth accumulation occurs. Finally, you want them to be good enough at money management that they fly off independently from your nest when they turn eighteen or so, to live fulfilling, enriched lives. You want them to have a strong appreciation of you as a parent, the skills you gave them, and the values you instilled in them.

So get to work and talk the talk. You can't talk the values if you don't walk the values, too. You have to act in synchrony with your words. Pass on those fiscal attitudes, imprint those financially relevant emotions. From the time your children are three years old refer to your own frugal behaviors with positive statements. For example, take pride in your old beater car. Call it your Urban Combat Vehicle. Make it sound cool. Tell your kids your car is paid for, a feature that saves you from making a car payment every month. You are saving that car payment in a college fund for them. Point out how much it costs to buy a new car every two years. Make each of those points into a story, a modern Fiscal Fable. Kids love stories.

Another example: being smart about avoiding a fee-based credit card. You, of course, did not plunk down $50 for the credit cards in your pocket, did you? Tell the story of how much it costs for credit cards that charge a fee and for the one you got free. Another Fiscal Fable.

Can you talk about the money you save on soda by not getting one from a machine? How about making Kool-Aid? How about water? Can you make a family adventure out of shopping at garage or rummage sales? Can you patch a pair of jeans with an iron-on patch? Can you pack a lunch instead of buying one? Do you talk about the savings in renting videos instead of going to the movies? How about homemade popcorn instead of theater popcorn? Your storybook is filling with fabulous Fiscal Fables.

Don't let your Fiscal Fables be myths. You have to walk the walk. Do you save every month? You want your children to. Are you living within your means? You'd better be if you want your children to. Are you accumulating wealth? Are you responsible about your own future? Do your kids know about it? Do you pay God first (charity), pay yourself second (savings), and use the rest to live on? You'd better if you want your children to. Your kids need to see your behavior and your attitudes matching your storytelling, your Fiscal Fabling.

Their job is to explore the world around them. Part of that exploration involves the boundaries their parents create around them. Those boundaries are mostly emotional and intellectual. Your kids have to push up against a boundary just to discover where each boundary is. Are you ready to define that boundary in a way that passes on an important truth? Be ready to define that boundary with a good Fiscal Fable, a lesson in wise money use.

Think about how you react to your young, impressionable children when they push a financial boundary. Let's say they want to go to the movies. You have a choice of reactions. You can say, "No, you can't go to the movies." Or you can say, "No, we can't afford a trip to the movies this month because I need to keep saving for your college fund and we can't afford both. But how about we set aside some money so that we can rent a video next week? Today I would like to play a game with you. How about Life or Monopoly?"

Stay engaged and stay concerned. Your children will lap up your love, your concern, and your wisdom.

You went through a lot of grief to learn the wisdom you have. If you really want your children to have a better life, help them learn early on the twentieth-century Fiscal Fables and folklore of sound money management. Achieving a better life for your children is not pampering them with indulgences but guiding them confidently with sound values and practices.

CHAPTER SEVENTEEN

WHAT'S THE LEAST I CAN DO
TO GET THE MOST EFFECT?

The Capitation Method detailed in the six Lesson Plans following this chapter is a compilation of the feedback I have gotten from different families who have tried some of these ideas. For some families the entire step-by-step program may seem a little complex, and they ask, "What is the least I can do that will have the most effect?" That is a fair question, and I address it last so you can get the whole overview before making decisions about what will succeed for your family.

I believe it is attitude that succeeds. If you create a common bond with your child as he or she starts down the path of discovery, you may find yourself with a teen who is eager to follow every step in the program. Congratulations. You are probably a standard deviation above most of the rest of us in energy and luck.

If you are looking for just the essence of this system, here are the two points I judge most critical.

1. Recognize that what you say and do every day is modeling behavior for your teens.

Your behaviors and stories, your Fiscal Fables, are your opportunity to imprint your teen with attitudes, examples, and recitations that create a culture. Because we live in a time of great change, it is likely that the culture you want your teens to inherit is different from the one in which you were raised. That means your efforts need to be all the more intentional and focused. What comes naturally out of your mouth may not be what you want your teen to believe.

Being intentional requires energy, particularly when you are up against the natural inclination of teens to challenge your authority. The energy I refer to is the will power you'll need to insist, for example, that your teens pack lunch every day instead of buying lunch at school. It is the energy to insist that your teens take food with them to a soccer tournament out of town instead of buying all their food in fast-food restaurants. It is the energy to refrain from rescuing your teens when they have blown every penny through frivolous behavior.

2. Understand that letting go of control is part of giving your teens responsibility for their finances.

Once the core behavior of managing their own money gets started, your teens are on their way. You will have to figure out together some mutually agreed-upon budget to cover their expenses, and you will have to decide which expenses are theirs and which are yours. It is up to you whether you tabulate their living expenses for six months or twelve, or just go with the flow and make a stab at it. Your teen will learn more if you calculate those expenses for a period of time. But if calculating those expenses is what's keeping you from getting started, your teen will nevertheless learn more by at least getting started.

It's likely you will glean the lion's share of benefit from this program even if the only thing you do is make your teens responsible for their own expenses for four or five years and give them a budget with which to manage that responsibility. The natural process of learning by error will be in place. They will make errors. Occasionally you will rescue them and occasionally you won't. But your giving up control will change the fundamental dynamics of who is responsible. The consequences are theirs. The connection between behavior and consequence will do the teaching for you.

Fundamentally you are changing the relationship between you and your teens. Instead of your deciding what they spend, you find that you have let go of that limiting supervision. They will have less reason to rebel and more reason to relate to you as the young adults they are becoming. This is the feedback I get most frequently from parents who have tried this method. And that kind of behavior is what the parents like the most.

What you will likely find is that some of the program works for you and some of it doesn't. But if you establish the pattern of sitting down once a month with your teen, you can follow a lot of it.

LESSON PLANS

❏ LESSON PLAN ONE
Creating a Clothing Budget
Grade Seven or Whenever You Can Start

❏ LESSON PLAN TWO
Using a Clothing Budget and Developing a Larger Budget
Grade Eight, Year Two

❏ LESSON PLAN THREE
Using a Larger Budget with an ATM Card
Grade Nine, Year Three

❏ LESSON PLAN FOUR
Getting Ready for a Checkbook and a Car
Grade Ten, Year Four

❏ LESSON PLAN FIVE
Paying for Expenses with a Checkbook
Getting a Credit Card
Establishing the Expenses of Driving and Insurance
Grade Eleven, Year Five

❏ LESSON PLAN SIX
Learning the Details
Planning for the Future
Saving for College, Retirement, and IRAs
Health Insurance
Starting a Family
Grade Twelve, Year Six

Note: To not slight either daughters or sons, gender references alternate between each Lesson Plan.

CREATING A CLOTHING BUDGET
Grade Seven or Whenever You Can Start

OBJECTIVES FOR THE YEAR: The first step is to introduce your kid to the idea of managing her "own money." The actions involved are: creating a budget, planning ahead, identifying needs and wants, learning to make independent decisions, figuring out what items fit into the Clothing Budget, finding alternatives to high-prestige spending, and writing a contract. Getting in the habit of saving and giving to charity should start at the very beginning if these are important values for you. These set the stage for future learning.

ADVANCED OBJECTIVE: Have your child discover and use the Internet to manage some expenditures. Consider how you can involve your child with the Internet each month.

Seventh grade is a good time to start working on these tasks, which require attention over time. Younger children often follow the rules their parents provide with too much obedience. They are not quite ready to try being independent. Some are, however. You know your child's maturity level. A thirty-minute session once a month means twelve sessions for the year. In reality I created only nine sessions a year because from time to time we all simply miss a month. You may be on vacation or too busy, some occasion may arise, or it just doesn't work out. The point is to keep at it. You will get to it. The learning involved in this book is all longitudinal and experiential. It cannot be learned from books. Attitudes are imprinted from example and from experience. The very nature of learning by experience requires long-term commitment. The premise of the Lesson Plans is that they mirror school years. Year one, however, may not start in September with a school year. You may choose a birthday or January 1 to start the process of developing a budget. So I list the first year's Lesson Plans loosely to allow for any starting date.

SESSION 1. Getting Started: Discuss the Ideas of Managing Your Teen's Own Money and How To Start By Making a Budget

SUPPLIES NEEDED

- Your credit card summaries for the last month with clothing charges on them
- Your checkbook with the same items
- Any other miscellaneous receipts for clothing
- Pencils and pads of paper

PROCEDURE

Ask your child, "How much do we spend on your clothes? Can you add up all the expenditures that we made for your clothing over the summer?" Make a list of categories of expenditures. Talk about the goals for the year, which are to save receipts, add them up, and keep a description of clothes purchased. Talk about how much you want her to save and how much to give to charity. Make the habits start from the very beginning.

REMINDER

Keep alert for opportunities to include your child in comparison shopping, choosing utility over fashion, and planning long-term goals. These ideas are the plot lines for good Fiscal Fables.

INTERNET LESSON—IF YOU HAVE INTERNET ACCESS AT HOME.

Find a site on the the Internet that gives an allowance calculator. Have your child look for it with key words "kids" and "allowance." If you do this on the search engine Google (www.google.com) you will find several. As of this printing there were at least three. You want your child to find something similar to www.laurelcfu.org/kidsmatter/money.shtml (one bank site that allows parents to give kids an allowance) or www.kidsmoney.org where you can calculate an allowance and have your child be given an automatic spending amount for each month for her own shopping on the Internet. Make sure that whatever site you go to has screens to limit online shopping to items you agree that your child may buy.

SESSION 2. Planning Ahead

SUPPLIES NEEDED

- Receipts from the last month's clothing expenditures
- A small, bound Budget book and a pencil
- Pad of paper

PROCEDURE

Ask your child, "What clothes expenditures have not been made yet? Can you see something coming over the horizon that will cost a lot of money?" Prepare a budget list for next month. Start keeping track of what you are currently paying for new school clothes. Save the receipts. Practice how to read cash register receipts and identify which ones apply to which items. Start a Budget book listing the different categories of clothes that you and your child decided on the previous month. Write headings on different pages of the Budget book for each of the categories of clothing you listed.

INTERNET LESSON

Did you set up an Internet account? Ask your child what she learned about the setting up process.

SESSION 3. Discussing Needs and Wants

SUPPLIES NEEDED

- Budget book and pencil

PROCEDURE

Winter is coming and big expenses for clothes are coming up. Ask your child, "What does your winter clothes budget look like? What new clothes do you need now? What are your total expenditures to date? What is comparison shopping? Can you bring in three prices on the same item from different stores (winter boots, mittens, coats, etc.)? Can you find the same type of functional item (winter boots) at different prices in one store? How about a trip to a mall, a shoe store, and a discount store? (Instead of calling it shopping, call it a field trip.) What do you need? What do you want? What comes first?"

Finally, "What is your best guess as to how much we have to spend on your winter clothes this year?"

Go on your field trip sometime this month.

SESSION 4. Comparison Shopping

SUPPLIES NEEDED

- The lists you made from comparison shopping last month
- Budget book and pencil

PROCEDURE

Ask, "How is your comparison shopping for clothes going so far? Where have you found the best bargain? Did you find a great sale? Or was it just a promotion to get you in the door?" Did anyone in your family go to a thrift shop, a reseller, or a Salvation Army store, or read a community newspaper for sale ads? Does your family use hand-me-downs? What is their advantage? How about another field trip to take some extra clothes your family doesn't need to a homeless shelter or a local thrift store?

Enter all your expenditures for the last month in your Budget book. Have you got something in every category yet? What is there still to purchase this coming year?

A possible extra-credit project: Get a catalog and have your child go through the process of selecting and ordering gifts for her friends or family, or clothes for herself for the coming holidays. Hang on to those receipts.

INTERNET LESSON

Can you have your child do an Internet search for some of the gifts she wants to purchase for the holidays?

SESSION 5. Midyear Evaluation

SUPPLIES NEEDED

- Budget book and pencil
- Previous month's receipts

PROCEDURE

Ask your child, "How did the winter clothes budget go? Have you kept inside your guess as to how much it would cost? Did it surprise you how much you needed? Are winter clothes costing more than you expected? Can you think of a way to make some clothes last a little longer?" Enter all your receipts and add up your totals. "What is the most expensive category for you? What is the single most expensive thing you have bought so far? How is your plan for giving and saving going?" Make sure you keep rewarding this behavior with praise.

SESSION 6. Midwinter

SUPPLIES NEEDED

- Budget book and pencil
- Doctors' bills
- Insurance statements
- All related receipts from a visit in the last few months to a doctor or a dentist

PROCEDURE

It is time to start making a list of clothes needed for summer, so think of planning ahead. Make a list of what is needed for the summer. Catch up on all your receipts for the first six sessions. Is there a new "most-expensive" category?

Ask your child, "What have you purchased over this winter that might be good for next year, too? Have any clothing articles been lost? How much did it cost to replace them?"

Go over any doctors' bills so she can see the charges as she moves through the insurance process. Tell your child how your health needs are provided for, where the money comes from, and how it's paid out.

SESSION 7. Spring Break

SUPPLIES NEEDED

- Budget book and pencil
- Receipts

PROCEDURE

There are lots of special vacations in March. Ask, "Any special trips? Will you require extra clothing for the trip? Is your summer list finished? Do you need some spending money on this trip? Have you earned it?"

Summer clothing is in the malls already. Have your teen go through a store and bring in prices on all the summer clothes she listed. Start talking about a Clothing Contract with your child. Try to identify how you are going to do this together. Talk with her about her being responsible for her own expenditures next year.

INTERNET LESSON

Can your teen find an article of clothing on the Internet that she needs to buy for summer? Have your child do so and order it.

SESSION 8. Real Spring

SUPPLIES NEEDED

- Budget book and pencil
- Summer clothes lists
- A rough copy of a Clothing Contract
  (See Basic Clothing Contract pp. 162–163.)

PROCEDURE

It is time to start summarizing. Ask, "What are your totals? What categories do they fit into? Did we think of all the categories?" Some of these categories are: sports outfits, good clothes, party clothes, play clothes, shoes, boots, special shoes, jackets, underwear, and socks. "How many other categories are there?"

Go over the Clothing Contract. Read it together. Plan on signing it next month.

REMINDER

Make a point of Fiscal Fabling this month. Tell your child a story about being frugal and choosing utility over fashion. Point out to her how you make your money choices. Include her in the decision process.

SESSION 9. Wrapping Up the Year

SUPPLIES NEEDED

- Clothing Contract
- Budget book and pencil
- Calculator

PROCEDURE

Say to your fiscally savvy teen, "Look at your summary in your Budget book. Add up the biggest items from the list and see how much they cost. How many months does it take to pay for a winter coat?"

Have your child add up a grand total of all categories on a summary page. Divide the grand total by twelve and set a monthly budget. Create a worksheet for use over the summer. I suggest starting on July 1 with her clothing budget. The reason is that summer clothing costs are low, giving your kid a chance to accumulate a month or two of extra money for buying new clothes for school in September. Think about creating some incentives such as, "Any money left over at the end of the year is yours."

INTERNET REVIEW

How did your teen's allowance go this year on the Web? What did your child purchase? What did she learn? Has it been useful for her?

End-of-Year Quiz for First-Year Kids

- Can you describe what a budget is?
- Can you list all the clothing items you need to buy for one year?
- What is the most expensive item in your clothing budget?
- How long do jeans last?
- Name three places to get clothes more cheaply than at the mall.
- Describe what the best part of learning about a budget was this year.
- How much did you save this year? How much did you give to charity?

Advanced Quiz

Enter all your budget items on a computer spreadsheet. Add them up and make separate sheets for each category. Figure out average expenditures each month for each category. Print it out and save it.

Your parents are very proud of you.

USING A CLOTHING BUDGET
AND DEVELOPING A LARGER BUDGET
Grade Eight, Year Two

OBJECTIVES FOR THE YEAR: Manage a clothes budget for a year while developing the data for a more inclusive Global Budget. Get and use an ATM card. These two processes happen simultaneously. Practice is what this is all about.

ADVANCED OBJECTIVE: Talk about saving for education or job training after high school. You, the parent, can tell your child what you have saved so far for him and how it has grown. Tell your child how you will work together over the next four years to help with his post-high school plans.

INTERNET OBJECTIVE: Continue to have him allocate a portion of his allowance to allow purchases off the Internet. This year consider teaching your child to get a financial calculator off the Web to plan savings for college.

Keep generating Fiscal Fables. Talk to your child at every opportunity that arises about how you make your money choices. Examples: Why do you buy gas where you do? What coupons do you clip? Why?

SESSION 1. Summer

SUPPLIES NEEDED

- New Budget book and pencil
- Calculator
- Receipts from the summer
- Basic Clothing Contract

PROCEDURE

Go back over the idea of the Clothing Budget and your teen's responsibility to purchase his own clothing. Review the Clothing Contract. Ask your teen to summarize how he has done on his budget so far over the summer. Create budget tables to follow over the year for his clothing purchases. By this I mean a page for each clothing category, with three columns, one each for the date, item purchased, and price. Then make a new section with pages for other categories you might develop this coming year, each with the same three columns.

This is the year he is on a contract for clothing. He is working with cash advances from a larger budget that is more inclusive of all his clothing expenditures. This is his first budget. He is taking responsibility for all his clothing needs. He is no longer considering just the cost of a single item; he is realizing how the cost of a single item makes an impact on what he has available for other items. If he spends $130 on a pair of high-top shoes, he will have little left over for the jacket he wants. This jump in responsibility is a big developmental step.

While your child is practicing this increase in responsibility, he also needs to be considering the next Global Budget, which includes even more items—all his personal belongings.

Explicitly state the need for your child to begin saving receipts for every expenditure that applies to his personal needs: toiletries, sports, gifts, recreation, pocket money, haircuts, music lessons, school supplies, etc. All should be written down in his new, more inclusive Budget book. Did your teen continue his savings habits from last year? What is he donating to charity? Keep talking about it, and rewarding him for it every month.

At the end of the session, **Pay him his first month's budget in cash.** Do cash for the first couple of months until you have firmly established the precedent of sitting down together each month.

INTERNET LESSON

Search for keywords, "College," "Expenses," and "Calculator" on a search engine. Google is clean and will take you right to a wide variety of calculators. Can you find one that will calculate the savings from making your lunch every day for one dollar instead of buying it for five dollars? Sites such as www.salliemae.com/ and invest.hartfordlife.com/calc/college.htm are both simple calculators you can direct your child to. What are your teen's plans for college? Have you discussed the role of saving for those plans with your teen? Discuss your goals together.

SESSION 2. Early Fall

SUPPLIES NEEDED

- Budget book and pencil
- Calculator
- Receipts for clothes and all other personal items
- Bank statement

PROCEDURE

Review the budget tables that you started in the Budget book. Fill in the categories for the year to date. Keep developing a list of other expense categories that your child could be responsible for in the coming year. Have him refine the list as you go along. He should have the hang of it by now from the previous year with the clothing list. Categories can be filled in as he buys items during the course of the year.

Fall is a big time for sports. Sports equipment can be pricey. Talk about it. Consider a comparison-shopping field trip to a sporting goods store and a reseller of used sports equipment.

Pay the budgeted cash when your session is over.

SESSION 3. Late Fall

SUPPLIES NEEDED

- Budget book and pencil
- Calculator
- Ads from newspapers about winter clothes
- A few holiday gift catalogs
- Bank statement

PROCEDURE

Your child is starting to consider buying a new winter coat with his own money. This is an expensive item that may need to have its cost spread over a few months. How do you get your child to do that? Is it time for another field trip to compare prices? This is his first exposure to saving up for a big item. He is imprinting on your attitudes. Your Fiscal Fables are very important here. Apply some energy to this process, because your attitudes will be observed very closely.

Enter his expenditures on clothing and your expenditures on other items. Have you discovered any new categories you did not think of before?

Your child is beginning to think about how much he needs to spend on holiday gifts. Have him guess what a reasonable estimate would be for his gift-purchasing budget. Talk about where that money should come from. Ask him to save all receipts so you can see how close to reality his guesses were.

Pay out your cash when the session is over.

SPECIAL PROJECT

Your "student" may have ordered items from a catalog last year. Reinforce that concept again. Compare catalog prices with local store prices for simple items. Compare the prices with newspaper sale prices, if applicable. Order gifts for a holiday gift exchange.

REMINDER

The holidays offer many opportunities for Fiscal Fables in line with your family's values. This is a crucial time to share your reasons for financial decision making. Ideas like "giving is more fun than receiving" become real when you make it fun by involving you and your child together.

INTERNET LESSON

Does your teen still have an online allowance? Can your teen buy something for the holidays on the Internet? What are the expenses of doing that versus going to a Walmart, Target, or other large discount store? Check out those companies on the Web and see what they have to offer.

SESSION 4. Winter Holidays

SUPPLIES NEEDED

- Receipts from gift purchases and from all clothing purchased, especially the winter coat
- Calculator
- Budget book and pencil
- Bank statement

PROCEDURE

Distracted by the holidays, your child may not focus too well on just clothing. Ask him to compare how he is doing on clothes with what he is spending the rest of his money on for the holidays. Review his estimates for gift spending with his actual expenditures. Finally, summarize his budget for all his other categories from the beginning of this school year.

Ask your child, "How was your catalog ordering project?"

SPECIAL PROJECT

Take your child along to return an unwanted holiday gift item.

SESSION 5. Midwinter

SUPPLIES NEEDED

- Budget book and pencil
- Calculator
- Receipts
- Bank statement

PROCEDURE

You now have six months of data on what his nonclothing expenditures have been. Take this time to add up everything in both his Clothing Budget, which he now controls, and his Global Budget, which he is planning for next year. What does his Global Budget look like? How much money does it add up to? Are you surprised? Is he? What is the most expensive item?

Have you taken the time to go over any insurance statements or health bills? It is only a few years until car insurance begins; now is a good time to expose your child to the idea.

How deep are you in credit card debt from the holidays? This is perfect Fiscal Fable material. If you talk the talk and walk the walk, your child will imprint on how you pay off that debt. The best model for your child's prudent behavior is your own this year. (Maybe next year?)

Remember, when you are in debt and still show your child that you continue to contribute to charity, you make a very strong value statement. Midwinter finds a lot of food pantries empty. If you are broke, can you take your teen with you to give some cans of food to a pantry? You are still committed to giving, maybe just not cash this month.

INTERNET LESSON

If you are beginning to talk about car insurance, this is the time and place to do research on costs. Can your teen find a site that compares car insurance costs? Your child knows the routine by now. Find a search engine he likes, type in "car insurance" and "teenager" and "compare," and see what shows up.

SESSION 6. Adjustment Month

SUPPLIES NEEDED

- Calculator
- Receipts
- Budget book and pencil
- Credit card bills
- Bank statement
- Medical bills

PROCEDURE

This is a good time to talk about how his Clothing Budget is going for the year. Help him add up his columns and consider the various sums. Has he spent all of his budget? Add up all his expenditures and see which category total is the largest. Talk about strategies to become creative and stretch the budget through to July.

Do you need to renegotiate the Clothing Budget? Ask your child. Also ask him what strategies he is most proud of so far this year for keeping within his budget.

Go over a medical bill again from the last few months.

It is time for another field trip. Go to the bank with your child this month and get him his ATM card. He now knows the connection between cash from your wallet and cash from your checking account in his ATM account. He needs to see you sign up for it at the bank. Confirm with the bank representative that you can turn the card off by calling if there is a problem with your teen's handling of the account. Also, make sure you know how to apply for replacement cards, what the costs of transactions are from other banks' ATM machines, what costs are incurred for going under the minimum limit, and if there are any charges for checking the account balance.

SESSION 7. Early Spring

SUPPLIES NEEDED

- Budget book and pencil
- Calculator
- ATM cards and credit cards
- Credit card statement
- Bank statement with ATM documentation

PROCEDURE

Review the bank balance from your teen's ATM card account. Discuss each of the extra fees he incurred for items such as checking balances and using outside ATM machines. Add those extra fees up. Tell him you plan to increase his ATM limits next year when he gets his Global Budget if he continues to be responsible. Can he remember what all his withdrawals were for? Did he save the receipts? Show him one of your credit card bills and explain how an expenditure made with a credit card comes back as a line item on the bill, which has to be paid off with real money. Make sure your teen can see a concrete flow of money from the credit card transaction to a payment to the credit card company. Concrete examples work.

Again, this is of intense interest to your teen. He's focused on your attitudes. He is imprinting on the seriousness with which you take credit card debt, the strategies you demonstrate for keeping track of expenditures and for limiting those you cannot afford. He catches on very quickly. This is a perfect chapter in the ongoing saga of your personal Fiscal Fables.

SESSION 8. Spring

SUPPLIES NEEDED

- Budget book and pencil
- Receipts
- Calculator
- ATM card
- Bank statements with ATM documentation

- A *new* ledger book for next year's budget that will cover all the new areas of responsibility for his Global Budget (sports equipment, gifts, personal toiletries, and so on)
- A rough draft of a Global Budget Contract based on the model in the last section of the book (pp.164–166)

PROCEDURE

Sums from this year's spending experience become the basis for next year's Global Budget. Add up the figures, including the adjustments you made to the Clothing Budget in Session 6. Put that information into a twelve-month format by making a grand total of all categories and dividing by twelve. (If you have only ten or eleven months of data, divide by ten or eleven.) Create next year's Budget book with categories for all the clothing categories and new categories of responsibility your teen will have generated with you over the year. You'll have an enthusiastic teen by now. He should be proud of his handling of his Clothing Budget, and having his Global Budget will make him even prouder.

Go over the rough draft for the Global Budget Contract with your teen. Make revisions and add any categories you and your teen have considered. Talk about coming to a conclusion next session about what total sum you will place in the account. One month of expenditures lies ahead that will finish off your totals.

INTERNET LESSON

Budgeting is a topic that has lots of Internet presence. Find some tips that help. What were they? Spending fifteen minutes on the Web will give your teen some good ideas.

SESSION 9. Summer Is Coming

SUPPLIES NEEDED

- Global Budget Contract in its revised form
- Last year's Budget book with its final sums and a pencil
- Calculator
- Final receipts for the year

PROCEDURE

Bring to a conclusion your spending plans for the summer. Getting started in July is a good time with few immediate expenses. Warn your child to keep track of his costs and to not spend everything at the amusement park. (He will anyway.)

Finalize how much you are going to put into the ATM account each month based on the monthly average of all expenditures totaled over the last year. (Your monthly range will be $150 to $275 if you buy new items as a family. Families with higher discretionary spending will have higher budgets as well. One family reported to me that they rely on hand-me-downs and summer garage sales and get along on $100 a month.) Put the sum in your corrected and finalized Global Contract. Sign it. Celebrate the signing. Save the pen.

You want the Global Budget to be in effect on July 1.

Remember to save all your bank statements and receipts over the summer. This can be a distracting time with summer vacations but a good time because of lower clothing costs. Perhaps your child will save some of his extra money and get a running start in September with his outlays for new clothing, sports equipment, and school supplies. (He probably won't. This is where he learns, so be prepared. It is very easy to spend that extra cash. Try to hold him to spending only his discretionary spending on discretionary things.)

INTERNET LESSON

Have your teen find two different financial sites on the Web that will give you a report on the savings started for college. Examples are easy to find. www.CNBC.com allows you to make a personalized stock ticker. CBS.marketwatch.com is another well-regarded financial news site. Have your teen visit both, look up the mutual funds Magellan and Vanguard Index 500, find their symbols, and look up the values for the day that your teen is searching. Now discuss how investing might be one part of a strategy for saving for college.

End-of-Year Quiz for Kids in Grade Eight

- What was the most expensive item in your budget? How long did it take you to save up for it?
- What idea did you have this year that saved you the most money?
- What time of year is the best time to go shopping for bargains, and what time is the worst?
- List all the categories in your budget that you are keeping for next year's budget.
- What can you do over the summer to make your budget stretch?
- What are you going to do with the extra money you have left over?
- How much do you spend on haircuts in one year?
- What is the total cost of cigarettes if you smoke a pack a day for one year? What could you buy with that money?
- How do you feel about what you contributed to charity this year?
- Have your savings grown?

Advanced Quiz

How are college savings plans going? How did your savings grow this year? Where is the money being saved? What are the benefits and risks of different kinds of savings plans, stocks, bonds, mutual funds?

If you started computer spreadsheets last year to keep track of expenditures, add to them this year and make comparisons.

USING A LARGER BUDGET WITH AN ATM CARD
Grade Nine, Year Three

OBJECTIVES FOR THE YEAR: Follow a Global Budget that your teen makes over the course of the year. Learn to delay gratification for large budget items but still purchase them. Learn to use "plastic" and see that it has real consequences and limits. Learn confidence in the value of buying based on cost and quality rather than on prestige and name brand. Become skillful at reading a bank statement. Keep giving to charity. Keep saving.

ADVANCED OBJECTIVE: Learn to use a money management program such as Quicken or Microsoft Money on a computer. Some kids are good with computers. The earlier you start introducing computer money management behaviors, the sooner your child will get used to them. If you have the time to make her Budget book in the form of a computer spreadsheet, do that, too. During the course of the year you can show your child how to make totals and include some statistical functions such as averages.

INTERNET OBJECTIVE: This year many kids are thinking a lot about learning to drive, even though it is over a year away. You are trying to teach long-term planning and budgeting. You also need to plan ahead for transportation needs for your teen. This year make the Internet Objectives be about cars and car insurance. Continue an Internet allowance and change it as you see fit to meet the needs of your child. Keep it as part of your Global Budget calculations.

This year is a good time to consolidate your teen's long-term planning behavior and help her learn to make independent choices. A Global Budget with an ATM card will be an exciting adventure.

Do not forget to continue to talk over with your child all the money choices you make and why you make them the way you do. The more Fiscal Fables you share with her, the more material she will have in her memory for future use. (Remember, you have to talk the talk and walk the walk.)

SESSION 1. Summer

SUPPLIES NEEDED

- Global Budget Contract
- New Budget book and pencil
- Receipts for all expenditures since last session
- Bank statement with the ATM card monthly summary

PROCEDURE

Ask your teen, "How have you done over the course of the first months with the ATM card? What do you like best? Did you have trouble keeping track of it? Do you need a wallet to carry it in?" Ask about special problems and triumphs. Show her how to review her bank statements. Create budget sheets that pick up where she was at the end of last year. Add in all the expenditures in all the budget categories you created, for example clothes, haircuts, school supplies, gifts, sports equipment, toiletries, special occasions, allowance/recreation. Ask if she has discovered any other categories. Remember to include music lessons, karate classes, transportation costs—whatever works with your family. Remind her about coming fall expenses and the need to save up for sports, winter coats, and new fall clothes.

Fill in the Budget book. Tell your teen you expect her to do it in the future, that you will no longer be filling it in. She should plan on bringing it to the session next month completely up to date.

ADVANCED OBJECTIVE

Visit five garage sales this month and see how many clothes you find that you could use. Bring back your list next month.

SESSION 2. Early Fall

SUPPLIES NEEDED

- ATM card and card statement
- Budget book and pencil
- Receipts
- Calculator
- Information relating to school or sports needs

PROCEDURE

Go over the bank's ATM statements again. Help your teen carefully read the statement so she knows to leave the base amount of your money in the account. Identify how much interest she earned and what sort of bank charges she accumulated.

Ask your child, "How do you read the ATM statement? Were you aware you spent as much as you did? What line means what? Where can you find out how much you withdrew? What did you spend that for? Do you have your receipts? What percentage of your budget are you spending on bank charges?"

Did your teen bring her Budget book already up to date? Go over pending big purchases again. Much as in eighth grade with clothing expenses, a Global Budget has a crunch in October. Your teen has several fiscal needs that are potentially high cost. Fall sports require expensive uniforms. In addition, winter requires expensive clothing, and there are gift expenses during the holidays.

ADVANCED OBJECTIVE

Design computer spreadsheets.

REMINDER

Your teen is doing lots of new stuff again. With this steep learning curve your attention to detail and focus on your child's needs is well placed. She is imprinting your attitudes like crazy. Make sure the ones you are demonstrating are the ones you want her to learn. Try to generate some Fiscal Fables about how you are careful with your ATM card, what mistakes you have made, and how you solved those problems.

SESSION 3. Late Fall

SUPPLIES NEEDED

- Budget book and pencil, or computer
- Calculator
- Receipts and bank statements
- A property tax or car insurance bill

PROCEDURE

Once your teen has the concept of a Global Budget, simulate a theoretical problem in which the bank account is overdrawn. Show her how to get out of being overdrawn.

Have your child brainstorm ideas on how to plan ahead for a big purchase. Write down some real strategies for spreading costs over a number of months. The practice of concretely planning ahead cements her abilities a little better.

Ask, "Have you returned an item that didn't fit or broke easily? What did you discover? What is the benefit of saving receipts?"

Show her your property tax bill or your car insurance bill. Tell her the Fiscal Fable about how you have been saving for these major bills all year through your escrow account at the mortgage company. Fables at this age have to be short and sweet. Three lines and you're done; four lines and you're out.

Did she bring the Budget book completely filled in and up to date? Tell her it's an expectation.

INTERNET LESSON

Revisit your insurance comparison sites on the Web. Start strategizing with your teen about how you are going to pay for her insurance costs when they come due next year. And have your teen visit an auto Web site and see what she finds. Some of your local dealers have Web sites. Can your teen find the cost of a three-year-old Jetta in your metropolitan area? www.webpeddler.com/ can help your teen get started.

SESSION 4. Winter Holidays

SUPPLIES NEEDED

- Budget book and pencil, or computer
- Receipts
- Bank statements
- Gift list

PROCEDURE

The holidays are distracting, as always. She will stress every budget. Can you reward the planning-ahead behavior your child did earlier in the year? Do you need to make her a loan? Go over the bank statements again until you are sure she has the process internalized. If your teen rolls her eyes, that means she has got the process down pat and wants to move on. In that case just ask for balances and interest earned. Have your child collect and label all receipts, save them in an envelope, and record them on her computer spreadsheets. Update her budgets in the Budget book or on the computer.

Have you gone over an insurance bill recently? Have you shared a medical bill? Did you show her the cost of car registration? Did you have to pay your property taxes last month? Has she seen those costs? Share them. Share your experiences.

SESSION 5. Midwinter

SUPPLIES NEEDED

- Budget book and pencil, or computer
- Bank statements
- ATM card
- All the holiday receipts

PROCEDURE

Remember to check and reward her for having her Budget book balanced before you sit down. This should be routine by now.

Paying off the holidays. Everyone does that. Compared to last year, you have been much more disciplined with your holiday money and have a good credit card bill to show your teen. Okay, this year tell the story about how you planned ahead for the holidays. Some of your Fiscal Fables may have more myth to them than you originally intended. How did your teen do with her planning and spending over the holidays? Celebrate her successes with her.

Has your teen blown her budget and spent every penny of her money—and yours, too? This is likely to have happened by now. If not, show her these words and congratulate her on being pretty responsible. Lots of teens squander all their money the first month or two on rather unimportant stuff. If she has spent all her cash, and yours to boot, try to balance firmness with reason. She has to pay you back. That means a month or two of enforced austerity. No consequences, no learning. Time to offer her a job around the house to teach her how to earn her way out of debt.

Do some housekeeping around the ATM technology. Look over her ATM cards. If your teen hasn't used a wallet to protect her cards, by six months these are pretty beat up—if not bent out of useful function. Go over with your teen how to obtain a replacement or report a lost ATM card. Make sure she knows how to get a credit balance with her card.

Show her on her bill how much it costs each time she asks the ATM machine for a balance. Show your teen how to call up the bank's twenty-four-hour information line to get the balance on her accounts.

SESSION 6. Adjustment Month

SUPPLIES NEEDED

- Budget book and pencil, or computer
- Receipts
- Bank statement
- Global Contract
- Your own credit card statement from this year
- Calculator

PROCEDURE

Ask your teen, "Is your budget going to fall short? How do this year's expenses compare to last year's?" Talk about real-life solutions. Tell a story about when you had to take out a loan and how long it took you to pay it off. Did you have to take on a second job? Did you have to work overtime? Compare the cost of a $1,000 loan from the bank and the cost of carrying that balance on a credit card. Look at the fine print on the back of your own statement to see the cost of interest rates for credit card balances. Calculate the interest rate of your own unpaid credit card balance. (Do not read it off the card statement; calculate it together with your teen so she sees the math.) Look up interest rates in the Sunday paper. Show her how a credit card is really an expensive loan if it is not paid off every month, but that it is a cheap way of carrying expenses for a month if it is paid off. Make sure she understands the cost of not paying off a balance. Her ATM card is not a credit card yet. She needs to understand the difference.

This is, again, all new material. It is timely and very relevant. Make sure she hears about how you made your mistakes and fought your way out. Spin the tale. Embellish it just a little. Kids love fables, fiscal ones, too.

INTERNET LESSON

If you are talking about credit cards and ATM cards, you can talk about credit histories. Can you use the Internet to find yours? Have your teen type in "credit" and "reports" on Google and see what she finds. You, the parent, may even want to order yours.

SESSION 7. Early Spring: Start of Planning for Next Year

SUPPLIES NEEDED

- Receipts
- Budget book and pencil, or computer
- Your checkbook and last account statement
- One month's supply of grocery store receipts

PROCEDURE

The next step in learning money management is handling a checking account. Your child needs to learn that. Ask her, "How does a checking account work? Where does the money come from? How do you keep track of it? How does it compare to an ATM card?" Go over each of these using your own accounts as examples.

Again, confirm that your child has entered all her Budget book items before you start. Bring her up to date with her own budgets.

ADVANCED PROJECT

Ask her to figure out from your month's supply of grocery store receipts how much you spent on food items for the family the preceding month. How much did that amount to per meal per person?

SPECIAL PROJECT

School field trip. These usually happen this time of year. Ask, "Were there extra expenses? Did you plan ahead? Where did the money come from?" Add it all up and make a balance sheet on income and expenses. Income, in this case, is the extra money you paid for the field trip.

SESSION 8. Spring

SUPPLIES NEEDED

- Budget book and pencil, or computer
- Calculator
- All of last month's receipts

PROCEDURE

Look at the budgets your teen made and the expenses she has had so far this year. Is she close to her estimates? In what areas did she spend more than what was expected? In what areas were those expenses under budget? Have her compare the two and try to figure out why the projected budget didn't make it. This is real life. Exploring the means by which you sort out these oversights helps program your child for the same kind of problem solving down the road.

SESSION 9. Last Session: Early Summer

SUPPLIES NEEDED

- Budget book and pencil, or computer
- Last receipts for the budget year

PROCEDURE

Go over your teen's end-of-year budgets and her adherence to them. How has she done? Celebrate. Ask, "Do you have any plans for the leftover money? Can you buy something fun with what you saved? Can you put extra money into college savings?"

Make sure she feels some rewards and some celebration.

End-of-Year Quiz for Kids in Year Three or Grade Nine

- Document the total interest received on your ATM account for the year.
- Document your most expensive budget item. What was its average cost per month?
- What is the cost-of-living raise you would need for next year to keep up with inflation?

- List the service charges you ran up on your ATM account last year. Could you have avoided any of them? How?
- Can you account for all the withdrawals from your ATM account and when you made them?

Advanced Quiz for Year Three

Did your spreadsheet budget agree with your projected budget? Show where it didn't meet your plans and where it did. How did you cope with the changes? What did you have to do to make up the differences? Can you format your spreadsheet to add up all the columns?

Internet Quiz

See if your teen can find your state's Web site for its Department of Transportation. Does your state have a graduated license law? As of early 2000 more than half the states do. Find the details of the graduated driver's license law on the Web site for your state. Print it out and read it so that both teen and parent understand it. You will appreciate knowing this ahead of time for next year.

GETTING READY FOR A CHECKBOOK AND A CAR
Grade Ten, Year Four

OBJECTIVES FOR THE YEAR: Hold the gains. Two years on a Global Budget consolidates the mature behavior that comes from your teen having taken responsibility for all his own expenses. Your teen should now have the hang of delaying gratification.

ADVANCED OBJECTIVE: Your child can start by paying lots of expenses using a checkbook. Learning to use a checkbook instead of an ATM card is a discipline that is hard to accomplish. The learning involved requires practice and familiarity with something that feels new. Have him try it out. To really be ahead, have him learn to keep track of his checkbook expenses with Quicken or Microsoft Money.

INTERNET OBJECTIVE: Expand upon your knowledge base from last year. This year learn how to find maps, find directions on those maps, and get across town using those maps.

> Buying a car for the teen driver may be in your budget. Looking for it on the Web should be part of your teen's lesson this year. Electronic banking on the Web when you set up your teen's checking account is another Internet goal.

It takes two years of planning and carrying out budgets for your teen to become confident about his planning abilities. That should be enough experience to give him confidence in the process. The coming year is the time to start consolidating what he has learned with more complex behaviors. A checkbook is on the horizon. A car is more than just a blip on his horizon!

Tenth grade is typically the year in which every American teen looks forward to the penultimate sacred ritual of passage into adulthood, the driver's license. (After that, turning eighteen and getting to vote seems like a letdown. Let's get real about teen priorities here. Getting the keys to the car is the real American rite of passage.) A driver's license is a photo ID. With a photo ID it is possible to obtain a checkbook. A car creates many "opportunities" for managing money wisely. (How's that for a positive spin on what is otherwise a black hole?) As you start to talk to your teen about car expenses (insurance, etc.), you will notice he is paying no attention whatsoever. Once more you need to let your teen learn by experience. By sixteen he will hardly be receptive to creative Fiscal Fables and lectures from parents. So your objective this year is to shepherd your child along the path of responsible care of a car and the expenses attendant to it, while still maintaining what he has learned about all his other expenses.

SESSION 1. Summer

SUPPLIES NEEDED

- Budget book and pencil, or computer
- Summer expenses
- Bank statement
- An application form from a bank for a checking account

PROCEDURE

Start the year by making sure your teen is really up to speed. Is he filling in his budget expenditures each month? If he has been in this process for three years, you probably have a savvy kid. Lay out your intended objectives for the year. What is a checkbook? Where does money come from to make a checkbook work? If you still have checks, do you still have money? Set the expectation that each month your teen will continue to list all his expenditures by budget category in his Budget book. Set up the categories using prior years' information. Add car insurance for the new driver if applicable this year.

INTERNET LESSON

Print out a map and directions for a trip you are taking this month. Do it door to door. Make your teen be the navigator. How accurate was the map? What were its failings? Yahoo has a Maps section in its menu if your teen does not know where to start.

SESSION 2. Fall

SUPPLIES NEEDED

- Receipts for expenditures since the last entry
- Budget book and pencil, or computer
- Bank statements for the last month

PROCEDURE

Review the bank statements with your teen. Show him how you enter items properly and how you balance the checkbook each month. Go over his own budget ledgers to make sure all items are being filled in. Work with him to make sure everything is being entered properly. If you use money management software programs on a home computer, show him how it works and how you can categorize items in the checkbook section. Ask your teen to consider the types of categories his checking account might cover. Introduce the idea of a debit card and how it works. Caution him as to the risks he takes if he uses it and loses it. The connection to his checking account is more abstract, but the debit card functions in the same way as a signed check.

Review the details of what has been expended in previous fall sessions. Ask your teen, "How are you doing on sports expenses? Do you see any problems a few months down the road? Are you prepared for winter and the holidays?" With any luck, this preparation on his part is now routine, and you need only inquire to make sure all is well.

SESSION 3. Late Fall

SUPPLIES NEEDED

- Budget book and pencil, or computer
- Bank statements
- Bravery

PROCEDURE

Make sure your teen sits down at home to keep up monthly accounting in his ledgers. This may feel boring, but it makes the process of allocating expenses concrete. Some kids do not need this tedious repetition. If you make your teen do this routine accounting for a year, he will have a very definite idea of how money is really allocated and where it goes. As this process becomes routine, it takes only ten minutes a month. Stop doing it with him if he does not need your help.

You're going on a field trip to the bank. Set up your trip to a bank to demonstrate how you open a checking account. Have a bank employee spend some time with you and your child describing the types of accounts the bank will set up for teens, and the charges associated with each one. Many tenth graders will not have driver's licenses yet but will be eager to know how a checking account works.

ANNUAL HOLIDAY ORDERING

Consider ordering gifts from a catalog as an annual treat. Have your child use checks to pay for his gifts.

FISCAL FABLE REMINDER

You might spin a yarn about how at one time you forgot how a checkbook worked and wrote too many checks. The famous line "Honey, we can't be out of money, there are still checks in the checkbook" is too universally true not to apply to you in some fashion. Tell your child about it. He will love hearing the humor. Without even knowing it, he will absorb the lesson that checks do not equal money.

SESSION 4. Winter Holidays

SUPPLIES NEEDED

- Budget book and pencil, or computer
- Checking account statement

PROCEDURE

There are lots of check writing opportunities during the holidays. If your teen has a checkbook by the holidays, encourage him to pay for all his gift purchases with checks instead of with cash. Aim for at least five checks to be written this month. Then, at your monthly money session, reconcile your teen's checking account. If you have a computer program such as Quicken or Microsoft Money, let your teen reconcile his accounts with you supervising. Look at the balances and service charges.

INTERNET LESSON

Find out how to balance a checkbook on the Web. There are lots of sites. If you have Microsoft Excel on your computer, there are good instructions for doing it in Excel at www.soita.esu.k12.oh.us/checkbook/checkbook.

SESSION 5. Midyear

SUPPLIES NEEDED

- Checking account bank statement
- Budget book and pencil

PROCEDURE

Reconcile another month's checking account. See how the holiday checks worked out. Was he able to write five checks? It takes several months to get the hang of using a checkbook when you are used to cash. Create the expectation that reconciling his checking account needs to be done routinely every month. Expect him to enter cash withdrawals in the check register, too.

Review the budget ledger book. Maybe all you need to do is just glance to be sure your child filled it in. Were the holidays and attendant expenses a separate category in his budget? Have you done several trips on Yahoo Maps with your teen by now? Has your teen mastered the process? How is he doing balancing his checkbook? Does your bank have Internet banking? Can you set up your teen to have access to his account on the Web?

SESSION 6. Adjustment Month

SUPPLIES NEEDED

- Your teen's bank statements

PROCEDURE

You need to demonstrate again to your teen how to call up the bank and get account information. You did it last year with the ATM account. Reinforce the behavior with the checking account. Appreciate his raised eyebrows. That means he knows what he is doing.

Ask your teen, "Can you do electronic banking at your bank? Do you know what that means? Call and find out. How do you stop payment on a check? Do you know how to report a lost checkbook?" Fill in the gaps of all the procedures you want your child to learn about banking. Show him how to call up his bank's twenty-four-hour hotline to get information he needs. Walk him through it.

ADVANCED OBJECTIVE

Have your computer-savvy teen figure out how to use electronic bill paying. If you are using it in some form, show him how you make your routine payments. Have him follow the calendar feature out a few months to see how the same payments show up routinely. Have him delete those payments and reenter them so he sees how the program works.

FISCAL FABLE OPPORTUNITY

You must have some good story to share about how you set up your electronic bill paying program. My own wild experience was a keystroke error on my part that electronically sent my electric utility payment to a stamp store in Indianapolis. As they say in the computer world, "Garbage in, garbage out." Lesson to teach: Precision with computers matters, especially when it's your money.

SESSION 7. Early Spring

SUPPLIES NEEDED

- Bank statements
- Budget book and pencil, or computer
- Latest car insurance invoice
- Safe Driving Contract (See pp. 167–168.)

PROCEDURE

Driving requires insurance. Have your insurance agent set aside a time to give your child a pep talk about rates, accidents, and the increases in charges when one gets a ticket or has an accident. If you have a savvy agent, he or she will know the risks of teen behaviors and the ways various states have tried to curtail those behaviors. Most states have graduated license laws. Look over an insurance application form as well as an auto insurance policy. Have your teen find out what "collision coverage" means. Discuss strategies about how to pay for it. What will he do if he has an accident—either a fender bender or a real crusher? Does your teen know what the meaning of "reckless endangerment of the public safety" means? Is it time for him to think about getting a regular job to pay for some part of his car expenses, such as gas, insurance, or meeting an entire car payment?

Go over the Safe Driving Contract with your child. Talk to him about your expectations for safe behavior and your expectations for maintaining good school behavior. See which of the safe driving issues fit with your sensibilities. Talk to your teen about what you want to add or delete from the contract.

Reinforce the budget ledger book. Have your teen add up all his expenses and see what they come to. Ask him, "What has been the most expensive item so far this year?" Car insurance!

SESSION 8. Spring

SUPPLIES NEEDED

- Checking account statement
- Revised Safe Driving Contract and pen
- Budget book and pencil

PROCEDURE

Balance another month of checking accounts. Finish up with your car insurance ideas. Make your teen practice paying for the insurance policy, even if you deposit money into his account to make the payment possible. Split up the cost of insurance so that you are adding the same amount to his account each month.

Sign the Safe Driving Contract. Make it a celebration. Bring out a cake. Balloons. This is a rite of passage that should be named and celebrated as such. (You can do the Safe Driving Contract and your car insurance behavior any time during the year that your teen turns sixteen and learns to drive. Be flexible with your timing.)

How has your teen done this year with his budget? Did he get behind in any category? Were there any new categories this year? Do you have to consider any changes for next year's budget? Does your teen have Web access to his checking account? How is his account balancing going? Do it every month.

SESSION 9. Summer

SUPPLIES NEEDED

- Bank statement
- Car insurance policies
- Budget book and pencil
- Calculator

PROCEDURE

It's time to summarize for the year. Total up budgets. Also add up all the costs of the family cars over a year. Think of all the costs besides insurance that it takes to make a car work (oil, tires, tune-ups, car washes, new mega speakers, etc.). How much is that per month?

Ask your teen to use only his checkbook this summer and to stop paying cash for anything. Over the summer you want him to continue to reconcile his checkbook with you each month, although you may not need to look over his shoulder so closely. Tell him you want him to show the statements to you only when he has completed reconciling them.

Sixteen years old—time to get a summer job. Have your teen plan on keeping all his pay stubs as well as records of his expenses over the summer.

End-of-Year Quiz for Kids in Grade Ten

- How much is your car insurance payment? How much is that per month? How does the total of your car insurance compare to your Clothing Budget?

- What is the cost of the family car? What's the total mileage you estimate putting on the car? How many cents per mile is that?

- What is the total cost of driving your car per mile? Base your estimate on the sum of the car purchase, insurance, gas, oil changes, and new tires every fifty thousand miles.

- Diagram the process of balancing your checkbook, starting with your current balance and ending with the bank's closing balance.

- What does each check cost to print? How much does it cost to pay each bill with a check?

Advanced Quiz

Print out reports with Quicken or Microsoft Money. Summarize expenditures for the year by category. Explore all the reports these programs can do for you.

Model the costs of driving a used car and a new car. What is the cost per mile of driving a new car? Add in insurance, gas, tires, oil changes, and $400 a year for repairs. Look up the same model that is three years old. What is the cost of driving that car per mile? Which is the cheaper way to go?

PAYING FOR EXPENSES WITH A CHECKBOOK
GETTING A CREDIT CARD
ESTABLISHING THE EXPENSES OF DRIVING AND INSURANCE
Grade Eleven, Year Five

OBJECTIVES FOR THE YEAR: Include in the Global Budget the cost of paying car insurance in addition to the other expenses started last year. Continue a Global Budget with a Budget book, an ATM card, a checkbook, and a debit card. Learn to recognize that a large, fixed-cost item such as car insurance may dwarf other bills but that it still must be accounted for—which is an important maturing step for this year. Practice making deposits into the checking account and balancing the checkbook, starting the first month and continuing all year. Practice keeping track of an ATM card and the withdrawals or point-of-service charges assigned to the checking account. Consider applying for a credit card.

ADVANCED OBJECTIVE: Have your teen balance her checkbook again this year with a computer program. Print out summary reports for the year by category. Have her use the planning feature of the program to do long-range planning for a large expense she anticipates, such as the purchase of a used car or post-high school education.

INTERNET OBJECTIVE: Start to plan for college this year. This requires beginning to look for colleges on the Web. The concept of long-term planning is made easier with easily accessible information. If you have not yet bought a car and plan to do it this year, that, too, can be part of this year's planning. Balancing a checkbook also takes repetitive practice. Your teen's bank may have online tools that help.

SESSION 1. Summer

SUPPLIES NEEDED

- Bank statements
- New Budget book for the year and a pencil, or computer

PROCEDURE

Start the year by reviewing how things went over the summer. Tell your child your expectations for the coming year. The assignment for this month is for your teen to organize her Budget book on her own. She needs to add the category of car expenses. Also have her write at least five checks to pay for purchases and make at least one deposit into her checking account.

Start paying a larger monthly amount into your teen's checking account to cover the cost of car insurance as the bill comes due. Insurance for a boy in the amount of $1,400 per year will require upwards of $117 a month added to the checking account. Parents may opt to have their teens work for that money.

FISCAL FABLE OPPORTUNITY

With car issues so prominent in your teen's mind, make sure you tell some stories about cars. Point out how expensive a new car is compared to the car you are currently driving (if that is true and your car is not a new, luxury SUV). Talk to her about the depreciation a car goes through in its first twenty minutes off the lot and in its first year of use. Tell the Fiscal Fables of how you chose the car you drive, and why. Select your stories to coincide with the values you want your child to develop. Although most of your previous opportunities for conversing with your teen occurred when you were driving in the car together, you may not have as many opportunities when she is driving on her own. Use the opportunities you have when you can.

INTERNET LESSON

Balance your checkbook on the bank's Web site.

SESSION 2. Fall: Reconciling Checkbooks

SUPPLIES NEEDED

- Bank statements
- Budget book and pencil, or computer

PROCEDURE

Go through the process of making sure all her expenditures are accounted for again. Learning these habits is so important that your teen must continue until it feels routine. That is why I keep repeating it. Show your child this paragraph if she rolls her eyes again. I am glad she is comfortable doing these steps. We can stop this review when she arrives at a session with it all done ahead of time. Meanwhile, have your teen show you the deposits made and the checks written this month. Reconcile the checking account.

Ask her about any extra charges or withdrawals on the debit or ATM card, and about checking account interest. Demonstrate how the amount in the account breaks down into all its requisite components. Plan on repeating the same assignment for next month. Have your child try to increase the number of checks for the month to seven. Have her practice projecting the amount she needs to save each month to add up to the cost of her car insurance.

This is homecoming season, with big parties and big expenses. Discuss who pays and with what. Has your child planned ahead, and does she have money left to spend?

SESSION 3. Late Fall

SUPPLIES NEEDED

- Bank statements
- Receipts
- Budget book and pencil, or computer
- Holiday gift catalogs

PROCEDURE

Balance the checking account bank statement again. Go over the process one more time. Save catalogs and have your teen order some gifts for the holidays that require her to fill out an order form and write a check. Remind her to add in shipping and any applicable sales taxes. Go over her Global Budget and her Budget book to help her decide what she can afford to spend on catalog items. She may not want your help. Don't be hurt—be proud of her independence.

INTERNET LESSON

Have your teen order some items on the Web for the holidays. Are you still providing for a Web allowance? How is that going? Have you been reviewing that? Does your site have a parental audit function where you can see what your child has ordered?

SESSION 4. Winter Holidays

SUPPLIES NEEDED

- None—assume the usual behaviors all happened on their own

PROCEDURE

Reward her good behavior of keeping up her Budget book and checkbook. Announce that you want to let her throw a holiday party to which she can invite friends. The proviso is that she have her Budget book up to date, her checkbook reconciled, and her fiscal affairs in order. Or maybe let her have a party just because you are crazy about her. Have her make a budget for the party. Add up all the expenses you are willing to pay for as a special event. Let your teen do the shopping. (Prepare to take out a second mortgage.)

SESSION 5. Midyear

SUPPLIES NEEDED

- Budget book and pencil, or computer
- Bank statements and check register

PROCEDURE

Time to catch up and balance the checkbooks again. How was the party? Was it in budget? How is this year's budget going? How is the insurance savings plan coming? Will your teen have money left after she pays all her budgeted items? Add car expenses, clothes, and essential supplies. The total should be smaller than her monthly income. If it is, she is living within her means. This lesson is worth repeating again and again. Ask your teen, "What are you saving for post-high school education? How do you intend to pay for it? Can you put away 50 percent of any money you make from a job for a post-high school education savings plan?"

INTERNET LESSON

Catch up on college planning and expenses. Visit the sites that you visited before and recalculate. Visit the sites of some of the colleges your teen may be thinking about to review their costs and compare that to your current state of planning. Have your teen do the data collection on the Web.

SESSION 6. Adjustment Month

SUPPLIES NEEDED

- None—just glance at the Budget book completed by your teen

PROCEDURE

Is the checking account reconciled?

Consider another field trip to the bank. The agenda this time can be loans and how to apply for them. You may be in the market to purchase a car for the family. Involve your teen in the process. While at the bank show her how to sign up for a safety deposit box. Discuss what items should be put in the safety deposit box. Have the bank officer go over all the other types of checking accounts, savings accounts, and other types of investment services the bank offers.

INTERNET LESSON

Look up car loans on the Internet. Have your teen find at least three vendors in your community and compare their costs for car loans.

SESSION 7. Early Spring

SUPPLIES NEEDED

- Sunday paper
- Receipts from one or two months of grocery shopping
- Bank statements
- Budget book and pencil, or computer

PROCEDURE

Make sure all your teen's bank statements are being reconciled. This should be routine by now.

Then introduce the concept of having your teen pay all her expenses next year for living at home. Yes, all. Make sure your teen understands that you are not necessarily expecting her to work to earn her share of all these expenses. Communicate to her that your wish is for her to become accustomed to handling larger amounts of money properly. At this month's session you and your teen are going to make a budget for room and board. Consider all the categories that your family is responsible for providing, such as shelter, meals, healthcare, special tuitions, and any other expenses you have. Prepare these categories together. You may wish to also build in charity and savings in addition to the other categories. The goal is to create a realistic, comprehensive budget in which nonnegotiable expenses comprise the majority of the budget and discretionary income for fun and frolic remains a tiny, residual amount. This contrast is a marked one compared to what most teens are used to working with, their discretionary income only, of which they can spend everything on fun and frolic, with nothing left for necessities.

Look up the cost of a month's rent in the newspaper. Find a neighborhood like your own and consider at least two people sharing rent. Then comb through your grocery bills and itemize all the expenses for food, and all the shared expenses for essentials such as light bulbs, toilet paper and laundry soap. Generate a monthly cost for rent, food, and essential supplies.

ADVANCED PROJECT

Have your teen figure from the above list what annual expenses are as a comprehensive sum. Have her calculate what she would have to earn a year to generate that sum, predicated on 30 percent taxes, 10 percent savings, at least 5 percent charity, and 10 percent discretionary spending in addition to her budget. Ask her to calculate how many hours a worker actually works in a year. How many dollars per hour does your teen have to generate to maintain the lifestyle to which she is accustomed? You might ask in a very low whisper, "And just how does this compare to the pay you are getting this summer? Shall we look at those college catalogs again?" Enough said. She will get the point. You have witnessed real-life sweat.

INTERNET LESSON

Have your teen look up the cost of an apartment in your community. Good words on your favorite search engine are the name of your city, "Apartments" and "Rentals." What are the costs of reasonable apartments in your city?

SESSION 8. Spring

SUPPLIES NEEDED

- Last month's Global Budget
- Examination forms for ACTs or SATs, college catalogs
- Budget book and pencil, or computer
- Bank statements

PROCEDURE

Assume the bank statements are in order. Check.

Talk again about making a budget that adds in room and board. Reinforce your desire to have the comprehensive Global Budget working for next year. Talk about her getting a job again this summer to pay for some of her expenses or to save for college.

Fill out college testing forms and response forms for all the colleges, sending out query letters you and your teen think might be appropriate.

INTERNET LESSON

Order catalogs from the colleges and universities your teen may be thinking about attending and that you want to visit with her this summer. Have your teen print out maps off her favorite Web map site.

SESSION 9. Summer

SUPPLIES NEEDED

- Checking account bank statements
- Budget book and pencil, or computer

PROCEDURE

Balance the checkbook for a final time. Finalize how much you are going to deposit into her checking account on July 1 to pay the expenses that you have worked on to date for her, including projected room and board. You may want to write an addendum contract for this, too. Again go over the items you would include in this budget to make sure you are all in agreement. Suggested categories: housing, food, car insurance, and car payment.

Your child does not have this money. You do. You are already spending it on her. Reassure her that you will pay her this money each month. You expect her to pay you back with separate checks for the cost of room and board. Room can be broadly interpreted to be a pure rent issue, or it can include the items listed below as an advanced project.

Reiterate to your teen that your goal is to demonstrate how much cash flow it takes to function, of which only a small amount is hers to spend on herself. Yes, you are serious. This is so important that you want her to really do this hokey exercise for a year so she gets the feel of it. Again, the gentle little whispered query: "Next year, you will be doing this for real, without us around. Where else will you learn?"

ADVANCED PROJECT

Then include these items in your comprehensive budget. Have your teen discover and calculate what her share would be of essential household supplies, utilities, phone, taxes. Have all the statements at hand to work on these calculations.

Finally, make some concrete summer plans for visiting the schools your teen might attend after her senior year. Make sure this planning occurs around your family's other intended summer activities.

End-of-Year Quiz for Kids in Grade Eleven

- Split your comprehensive budget into its categories. Which is the largest?
- Define some hidden costs in your checking account that you discovered this year.
- What do you do when you lose a check?
- Why do you save checks?
- Why do you keep bank statements?
- How much does a loan for a car cost you over the life of the loan?

Advanced Quiz

Use your computer program to generate all the new categories you added to your comprehensive budget: rent, food, supplies, utilities. Print out reports detailing the total costs incurred during the course of the year. Set up automatic monthly withdrawals or payments back to your landlord (Mom and Dad).

How are savings for college going? Can you run the planning programs in the financial software? Project how much college is going to cost you at each place you are thinking of applying to. What will you have to save, earn, or borrow, according to your projections, for each college you apply to?

LEARNING THE DETAILS
PLANNING FOR THE FUTURE
SAVING FOR COLLEGE, RETIREMENT, AND IRAs
HEALTH INSURANCE
STARTING A FAMILY
Grade Twelve, Year Six

OBJECTIVES FOR THE YEAR: Have your teen paying his own way the entire year. He should be experiencing enough cash flow into and out of his account to simulate the realistic costs of paying for room and board, clothing, insurance, transportation, and food, using what is left over for fun. Finally, there are other issues he has not yet thought about that need to be considered: getting health insurance, starting his own family, and saving for his own retirement, to name a few. This is the year to think about these and try to estimate what the costs will be.

ADVANCED OBJECTIVE: Have your teen apply for a credit card this year and make at least three charges a month without incurring a penny of interest. Have him use a spreadsheet to calculate a budget for raising a child. Remember inflation. Have him start an IRA.

INTERNET OBJECTIVE: Your teen should be pretty Web savvy by now. This year is a good year to keep reinforcing that your teen should use the Web to find information on a routine basis. And keep using the skills he has developed so far. Financial information and planning information is abundant on the the Web. If you can open an IRA this year for your teen, it may be worth your while to help him by starting it with the money you put in. Order the information from the Web. Virtually all the large mutual fund companies, such as Vanguard, Fidelity, Janus, T. Rowe Price, etc., have Web sites. Order forms over the Web together with your teen. Try to set it up so that he has access to the information over the Web.

Having a senior in high school is a special experience for parents. Evidence that your teen exists is limited to such subtle clues as pizza crumbs on the kitchen counter with an oven set at 375 degrees and the trash cover off with a frozen pizza cardboard box stuffed halfway in. Of course, the oven is still on. Did you hear the garage door open at 12:30 last night? This is evidence that your teen is doing the work he needs to do. He is separating from you and learning to be independent. If he came home at 8:30 P.M., just before you went to bed, he would have to talk to you and you would have the urge to make suggestions about how his life should be run. After midnight, he is safe.

Sound familiar? This year is one in which your hands are increasingly off of his affairs. The Lesson Plan that follows is primarily for those families that are still relating in a more day-to-day fashion with their teens. Some high school seniors are so much on autopilot that you might have difficulty pinning them down to a monthly session. During the senior year the prospect of college expenses will seem overwhelming. College admission forms are equally daunting. This is where your child needs you, and your availability to assist is an opportunity to strengthen your relationship. Use whatever opportunity you can with kindness.

SESSION 1. Summer: Get a Job

SUPPLIES NEEDED

- New Budget book containing new categories for room and board, and pencil
- Your recent health insurance premiums
- This week's Sunday paper
- All of last month's grocery receipts

PROCEDURE

Establish that this year you want your child to pay you for room and board. Do you have last year's calculations for your teen's room and board payments? Including his budget for clothing and all his other incidentals? If not, do these calculations first. I recommend taking a Sunday paper real estate section to learn the rents of apartments in the area. Have your teen add up all your grocery bills for a month and divide by the number of members in your family. You need to start depositing this amount into his checking account each month. Then he can pay it back. Sounds hokey, I know. Just do it. It's new turf for him. Experience and routine make for good imprinting.

Finally, ask your teen to bring to the next month's meeting his balanced bank statements, showing at least five checks written for various expenses.

SESSION 2. Fall: College Expenses

SUPPLIES NEEDED

- Budget book and pencil, or computer
- Bank statements
- A current college guide with comparative expenses in it
- Financial aid application forms

PROCEDURE

First, go over his bank statements and make sure he has balanced everything properly. Did his five checks work out? Did he pay you for room and board?

Talk about college costs and how to apply for financial aid. Have your teen make a budget to cover paying for the cost of college. Review a college guide that compares the costs of tuition, room, and board at various colleges. You may have already visited some of these and gotten a sense of what the costs might be.

The financial aid forms may take many more sessions. Do not let this slide too long. There are many books and sources advising how to apply for financial aid. You may want to incorporate this information into your monthly money talk. While this is such a large topic that it is beyond the scope of this book, the exercises in this book will, I hope, provide the underpinning for doing this planning with your teen.

Have him expand his budget one more time to include the cost of quarterly or semiannual tuition at college or post-high school vocational training. Make another page in his Budget book to reflect the loans he may need to take out. Use red ink. Talk about how his long-term income prospects increase with each year of school after high school (between 10 and 15 percent per year).

INTERNET LESSON

Have your teen find how much more income a college graduate earns than a high school graduate.

SESSION 3. Late Fall: Savings and Investment

SUPPLIES NEEDED

- Bank statement
- Budget book and pencil, or computer
- IRA application form from a major investment company

PROCEDURE

Review the bank statements for your teen's checkbook. Did he write four checks again this month? Ask him how he feels about the costs you are charging him for room and board. Can he make a comparison between the costs of eating out at a fast-food place versus preparing his own meals?

Review his budget ledgers to see if your projections are on track for this year. His financial behavior is by now five years old and pretty routine.

It is time to talk about IRAs, Keogh plans, pension plans, and other long-term savings tools. Calculate the power of fifty years of savings versus thirty years of savings. Talk about investing at least $50 a month for the rest of his life. Show him the advantage of tax-protected savings. You can do these projections on most computer programs, such as Quicken or Microsoft Money. He can see that saving $50 a month for fifty years with a 10 percent return makes for $187,000. This is a great time to start an IRA for him with some of his hard-earned cash from his summer job (small, but symbolically important). You may need to help with the initial minimum.

You might play a game of allocating to your young adult $100,000 in phantom money, which he must invest in the stock market or in mutual funds and follow for the course of one year. Ask your teen to find out what "no load" means. Ask him to find out what dollar cost averaging means.

INTERNET LESSON

Ask Google or Yahoo or Lycos, etc., what "dollar cost averaging" means. What colleges has your teen narrowed his choices down to? What information on the Web might help him compare the colleges to each other?

SESSION 4. Winter Holidays: More on Saving and Investing

SUPPLIES NEEDED

- Bank statements
- Budget book and pencil, or computer

- IRA form from last month
- The Sunday paper, and a recent financial magazine (such as *Money, Kiplinger's, Smart Money,* etc.).

PROCEDURE

Review his bank statements again.

Follow up on last month. Ask your teen, "What do 'no load' and 'dollar cost averaging' mean?" Look up stocks in the newspaper and see how your child's simulated portfolio is doing. Assign your teen to review at least one business section from a newspaper each month and circle his phantom investments. Have him calculate his rate of return. Talk about risk and volatility in the market.

SESSION 5. Midwinter: Buying a Home

SUPPLIES NEEDED

- Bank statement
- Sunday paper
- A free real estate tabloid from the supermarket
- Your home's tax assessment for last year

PROCEDURE:

Review your teen's bank statements. He should be on track.

It's time to talk about real estate. Look at the newspaper and the costs of renting. Then review the real estate tabloid and look at the costs of purchasing a starter home. Go over mortgage tables in the Sunday paper to see what mortgage rates are. Calculate a 10 percent down payment on your own home based on last year's tax bill. How long would it take to save up for such a down payment if your teen put away $200 extra a month? How do mortgage costs compare to rent? What does inflation do to the value of a home? What are closing costs? What is title insurance?

INTERNET LESSON

Have your teen look up homes for sale in your community on the Web. Nearly every real estate company has a Web site. Ask your teen what his expectation for housing is. Is he aware of what a down payment might be for a first home?

SESSION 6. Late Winter: Charitable Giving

SUPPLIES NEEDED

- Costs for the college choices he has narrowed down
- Bank statements
- Budget book and pencil, or computer

PROCEDURE

It's time to focus on real values. Your kid's friendships in school are coming to a new phase or a possible end as graduation arrives and he considers moving to a different community for school. Talk about how money is just a means of getting by and paying the rent. Ask your teen, "What are your real values?" You may be surprised to hear his answers. He will likely list friendships, integrity, goals, relationship to a higher power, responsibility for the world. Handling money well allows some things to be easier, but not everything.

Can he build into his budget a commitment to give something to a cause bigger than himself? Does it have to be money that he gives? Can he give his time, his energy, his ideas, his enthusiasm, his commitment? When he is broke, enthusiasm may be all he can give. Can you tell a Fiscal Fable about charitable causes you have been involved in?

SESSION 7. Early Spring: Employment-Related Benefits

SUPPLIES NEEDED

- Budget book and pencil, or computer
- Bank statements
- The Sunday paper's employment section

PROCEDURE

Reconcile your teen's bank statements.

Look through the employment section of the paper together. See if you can find a job that might be of interest to him when he graduates. Look at what benefits are listed. Talk about employee benefits: Keogh plans, pension plans, disability insurance, vacation, continuing education, company cars.

Introduce this conversation now so he has some context in which to think about jobs as he approaches the world of employment. By having this conversation now, you open the door for him to come back to you later. Have you ever been disabled for a period of time? This is a great Fiscal Fable opportunity. Tell your teen about it. Did you have savings to cover your living expenses for that period of time? How much do you currently have saved for an unforeseen calamity? The financial gurus recommend having six months of living expenses set aside in an easily accessible account. What kind of saving effort does that require? What is your teen's total monthly living expense? The likelihood of being disabled for six months during the course of his lifetime is over 50 percent.

It is even more likely in his lifetime that he will experience at least one job being discontinued for one reason or another. Do you have a Fiscal Fable to tell about when you changed jobs? How long were you laid off? Did you have to move? Talk about other ways of getting through a crisis, such as by borrowing money. Can you live on your credit cards? What does credit cost compared to taking out a bank loan or a home equity loan? What does bankruptcy mean?

Do you need to review college expenses again? Has your teen been accepted? Did you have a party? Congratulations are in order!

SESSION 8. Spring: Health Insurance/Life Insurance

SUPPLIES NEEDED

- Your health plan description of benefits
- Your life insurance statements

PROCEDURE

It's time to talk about health insurance choices. Define the terms: deductible, out-of-pocket expenses, HMO, primary care physician. Can you tell your teen how to get free advice on the Internet or from a local Call-a-Nurse? When should you call your family doctor and when should you call 911? Does your teen know what coverage he needs for routine health maintenance? Does he know about getting a tetanus shot every ten years and having his blood pressure checked every other? Does he know about sexually transmitted diseases? Where would he go to get help, and how would he pay for it? Talk about it now so he has some minimal framework. No one else will do it for him.

Ask if he understands what life insurance is for. When should one purchase life insurance? This is another opportunity for Fiscal Fabling. Talk about your mistakes and what you have learned over the years. It seems most everyone has some story to tell about life insurance. Does your child know those stories so he can learn from your mistakes? Does he even know how to buy life insurance? Tell him. Show him your statements. Can you show him your whole life policy and what its cash value is now? Do you have feelings about this policy that you want your teen to know?

How is the stock portfolio doing?

INTERNET LESSON

Have your teen do some life insurance comparisons. The Web has leveled the playing field. There are large brokerage houses that compare insurances for you. Find one and find the cheapest term life insurance for your teen's age.

SESSION 9. Summer and Graduation

SUPPLIES NEEDED

- A cake

PROCEDURE

He made it! Nothing but congratulations this session. Make some sort of awards for the CEO of Me, Inc. Your child is graduating from high school with more financial savvy than most adults ever acquire. He is ready to launch into the complex world, prepared with a foundation of tools most families have never been able to give their kids. Good work to you, too!

No End-of-Year Quiz

School is out. Good luck!

CONTRACTS

❏ Basic Clothing Contract

❏ Global Budget Contract

❏ Safe Driving Contract

❏ Car Use Contract

CONTRACTS

Although it is not absolutely necessary to use written contracts, using them gives you a reason for some very intentional behaviors you may not otherwise do. For example, the exercise of writing everything down forces you to consider just what it is you are talking about. You clarify your language. You define the limits and boundaries of your expectations. You can even put in escape clauses, such as a paragraph on the consequences of pushing boundaries.

By having your boundaries defined in writing and agreed to ahead of time, you have a means of making the boundary stick. Without consequences, learning is often subverted. And if you cannot make the boundary stick, you are vulnerable to the games teens learn to play: "I spent all my money on presents, which is why I can't get new shoes for basketball." The real world runs on contracts. Learning to cope with the real world starts with little consequences in the safe world of a loving family. But you still need them. It is hard to make your teens deal with the consequences of their actions unless you have been very explicit ahead of time. Contracts force you to become explicit.

Here are some examples written in kids' language. Feel free to copy, change, or rewrite to suit your needs. They are also available for download on my Web page, www.capitateyourkids.com. The more you and your teen change the language together, the more likely you will be to succeed at defining and sticking to boundaries.

161

BASIC CLOTHING CONTRACT
CONTRACT BETWEEN [CHILD'S NAME] AND MOM AND DAD
FOR [CHILD'S NAME] CLOTHING BUDGET FOR [YEAR]

PURPOSE

The purpose of this contract is for each of us to write down what we expect from each other and what is allowed in the coming year.

MOM AND DAD'S RESPONSIBILITIES

1. We agree to provide $____ for the use of [Child's name] for the purpose of buying the clothes listed below for a period of one year: ____ to____. This money will be delivered:
   (a) as needed,
   (b) monthly in the sum of $____, or
   (c) in one lump sum of $____.

2. We agree to provide transportation to reasonable sites for shopping at a reasonable frequency, upon fair and advance notice by Child, not to exceed ____ times a [day/week/month].

3. We agree not to interfere in choices of clothes unless Child agrees to or asks for an adult consultation.

4. We agree to help with ideas for alternative clothing sources, such as rummage sales, newspaper ads, sewing, hand-me-downs, etc.

5. We agree to provide the funds to meet the minimum deposit requirements of the ATM account at the bank that allow [Child's name] to deposit and withdraw money with the ATM card interest free.

6. We agree to assist Child in learning how to use an ATM card, how to read bank statements, how to get replacement cards when the original is lost, and any other banking information that may be needed to maintain Child's financial accounts.

CHILD'S RESPONSIBILITIES

1. I agree to limit, in all good faith, the cost of clothing to $____ for a period of one year: ____ to ____.

2. I agree to shop for reasonable values.

3. I agree to keep all receipts and tags from clothing.

4. I agree to dress with reasonable neatness for special occasions such as church or synagogue, school parties, weddings, birthday parties, etc., and to obtain appropriate clothes for such occasions.

5. I agree to not ask for more money for extra clothes.

6. I agree to make a checklist and plan ahead for clothes needed later in the year.

7. I agree to try not to shop out of envy for what other kids have.

8. I agree that the items included in the clothing list shall be all: underpants, bras, socks, pantyhose, T-shirts, tops/blouses, shirts, skirts, dresses, jeans, pants, shorts, dress pants, dress shoes, sneakers, sandals, winter jacket, windbreaker, winter gloves, scarf, winter hat, winter boots, sweater, swimsuit. Furthermore, any formal clothing needed for parties or religious wear shall be included as well.

9. I agree not to withdraw money from the ATM account below the baseline amount of $____ needed to establish the account.

10. I agree to pay bank fees for any withdrawal below the required minimum balance.

11. I agree that the baseline money belongs to Mom and Dad.

12. I agree to go over the bank statement with Mom and Dad each month and explain what the money was withdrawn for.

13. I agree to take care of the ATM card so it does not become lost or damaged. If replacement is needed because of loss or damage, I agree to pay the cost of replacement.

MISCELLANEOUS AGREEMENTS:

1. Any money left over shall belong to [Child's name].

2. Any inadvertent major loss such as the loss of a suitcase or a major theft shall be "insured" by Parent. Parent promises not to let Child be seriously harmed because of the lack of proper clothes.

3. Both parties agree that if any item in this contract cannot be met, the contract may be reopened for amendment. Doing so shall not prevent the rest of the items in the contract from being in force.

_____   _____
CHILD SIGNATURE   PARENT SIGNATURE

GLOBAL BUDGET CONTRACT
CONTRACT BETWEEN [CHILD'S NAME] AND MOM AND DAD
FOR [CHILD'S] GLOBAL BUDGET FOR [YEAR]

Note: This contract is a little more complex. Some parents choose to stipulate that money will be paid only upon completion of a monthly "fiscal session" or "audit" or bank statement review. That can be added and is mentioned to give the reader some ideas about how to use the enclosed contract for a starting point.

PURPOSE

The purpose of this contract is for each of us to write down what we expect from each other and what is allowed in the coming year.

MOM AND DAD'S RESPONSIBILITIES

1. We agree to provide $____ for the use of [Child's name] for the purpose of buying the items in the categories as listed below.

2. We agree to deliver/deposit this sum on a monthly basis or in a lump sum directly into the account established at the bank.

3. We agree to not interfere in choices of items unless Child agrees to or asks for an adult consultation.

4. We agree to help with ideas, helpful suggestions, and assistance with planning ahead.

5. We agree to provide the funds to meet the minimum deposit requirements of the ATM account at the bank that allow [Child's name] to deposit and withdraw money with the ATM card interest free.

6. We agree to assist Child in learning how to use an ATM card, how to read bank statements, how to get replacement cards when the original is lost, and any other banking information that may be needed to maintain Child's financial accounts.

7. We agree to pay for:
   - Shelter (housing, electricity, heat, bed, sheets, desk, towels, etc.)
   - Food (anything in the way of food at home, school lunch supplies, and food for special trips)
   - Medical (all medical and dental care, including doctor visits, prescription drugs, glasses, braces)

- School supplies (special projects, field trips, etc.)
- Special school trips (by negotiation)
- Music equipment (radio and CD player are in the home)
- Household items (generic soap, toothpaste, shampoo, detergent, toilet paper)

CHILD'S RESPONSIBILITIES

1. I agree to limit, in all good faith, the cost of all items in this Global Budget to $____ for one year: ____ to ____.

2. I agree to shop for reasonable values.

3. I agree to keep all receipts and tags from all purchases and to keep track of them in my Budget book.

4. I agree not to ask for more money for extra purchases.

5. I agree to make a checklist and plan ahead for expensive items needed later in the year.

6. I agree to try not to shop out of envy for what other kids have.

7. I agree that the items included in the Global Budget shall be those items that I shall be completely responsible for. Check all that apply:

CHILD PAYS FOR

— All clothes (as indicated in the Clothing Contract from the preceding year or below)

— Sports equipment

— Presents for holidays

— Haircuts

— School supplies—notebooks, pens, pencils, paper, binders, backpack

— Toiletries (except generic soap, toothpaste, shampoo)

— Weekend parties, movies, pocket-money-type stuff

— Clothing and supplies for proms

— Fancy toiletries and makeup

— Extra food (a fridge full of lunch material will be provided for me to pack lunches; if I want to buy lunch at school, that's my business)

— Big things that affect the family

8. I agree not to withdraw money from the ATM account below the baseline amount of $____.

9. I agree to pay bank fees for any withdrawal below the required minimum balance.

10. I agree that the baseline money in the ATM account belongs to Mom and Dad.

11. I agree to a fiscal review session each month in which I will go over the bank statement with Mom and Dad and explain what money was withdrawn for. I agree that not meeting is grounds for suspending the ATM card.

12. I agree to take care of the ATM card so it does not become lost or damaged. If a replacement is needed because of loss or damage, I agree to pay the cost of replacement.

MISCELLANEOUS AGREEMENTS:

1. Any money left over shall belong to [Child's name].

2. Any inadvertent major loss such as the loss of a suitcase or a major theft will be "insured" by Parent. Parent promises not to let Child be seriously harmed because of the lack of proper Global Budget items.

3. Both parties agree that if any item in this contract cannot be met, the contract may be reopened for amendment. Doing so shall not prevent the rest of the items in the contract from being in force.

| _____ | _____ |
| CHILD SIGNATURE | PARENT SIGNATURE |

SAFE DRIVING CONTRACT
CONTRACT BETWEEN [CHILD'S NAME] AND MOM AND DAD
FOR [CHILD'S] SAFE DRIVING FOR [YEAR]

Note: Though not strictly part of a budget, the concept of privilege tied to satisfactory performance of other agreed-upon behaviors is intrinsic to this book. The freedom of driving is so important to teens that it is equally important to have that freedom tied to responsibility.

PURPOSE

This agreement is written to identify those features of safe driving that the Driver, [Child's name], agrees to follow. The features named here are not intended as a complete list but as examples of the values of respecting other drivers, safeguarding self and others, and using a vehicle for safe transportation.

CHILD'S RESPONSIBILITIES
1. I agree to obey all traffic laws to the level of reasonable safety (posted speed limits not to be exceeded by more than 5 mph).
2. I agree not to allow any other party to drive any vehicle with which I am entrusted without explicit permission from my parents. Furthermore, I agree to ask for the use of the vehicle and not use any vehicle without prior negotiation/notification of my parents.
3. I agree not to transport more than two other people at any one time.
4. I agree not to use alcohol or other drugs or permit them to be used while I am driving a vehicle with which I am entrusted.
5. I agree not to react to other drivers' bad driving habits and behaviors.
6. I agree not to race other drivers.
7. I agree to always wear the seatbelt provided, and to ask that all my passengers use theirs.

8. I agree that if my grades fall below 90 percent/B+ [adjust for different abilities of child] in all courses not of an advanced placement (AP) nature, I will not drive until they exceed____ in any subsequent quarter.

9. I agree that I will pay the cost of any ticket myself.

10. I agree that if I have any traffic infraction or other ticket, or if I am at fault in any accident that causes damage to my car or another's car, I will relinquish my driving privileges for [six] months.

11. I agree that I will pay for any incremental increase in cost applied to the family's auto insurance resulting from any ticket or accident I have. I also agree to pay the cost of any damage to my or another's car not covered by the family's auto insurance.

12. I agree to report any ticket or accident to my parents.

13. I agree to drive defensively, always anticipating the poor driving of others. I will not tailgate.

14. I agree not to use the vehicle to play any sort of games, such as "chicken," at railroad tracks. I will use this vehicle, or any other vehicle that is offered to me, for the purpose of safe transportation only.

15. I agree to obey a driving curfew and not drive after 12:00 midnight or before 6:00 A.M. unless my job requires it.

16. I understand that my family loves me and has designed this contract for the purpose of building safe driving habits and strong trust relationships with those who want my safety more than any other item in this contract.

_____   _____
CHILD SIGNATURE   PARENT SIGNATURE

CAR USE CONTRACT

CONTRACT BETWEEN [CHILD'S NAME] AND MOM AND DAD
FOR [CHILD'S NAME] DRIVING PRIVILEGES FOR [YEAR]

Note: If you assist your teen with getting a car for her specific use, this contract expands your expectations in her responsibilities in caring for the car.

MOM AND DAD'S RESPONSIBILITIES

1. We agree to purchase a safe operating vehicle with adequate safety features, which include airbags, seatbelts, and appropriate tires.

2. We agree to pay for a base insurance policy for coverage against liability and collision.

3. We agree to maintain an account for all maintenance costs in a fund designated for such.

4. We agree to provide financial backup for repairs and large maintenance fees.

5. We agree to provide guidance and direction for legal affairs, licensing, etc.

CHILD'S RESPONSIBILITIES

1. I agree that driving the car is a privilege attendant on all prior rules and agreements made in this family about safe driving.

2. I agree to pay Parent $_____ a month to be put into a fund to provide all maintenance fees such as tires, repairs, and oil changes. Any surplus in such fund shall be considered payable to me upon graduation or termination of this agreement.

3. I agree to perform routine maintenance on the car—3,000-mile oil changes, car washes periodically, waxing at least once a year, etc.

4. I agree to pay for all gas and oil.

5. I agree to participate in shoveling the snow to keep the driveway clear during winter.

6. I agree to keep the car doors locked when not parked at home or at a friend's house.

7. I agree not to use the car to leave school when school is in session.

8. I agree to keep a curfew of 11:30 P.M. on weekends and 7:30 P.M. on school nights unless special permission is obtained.

9. I agree to notify parents of my whereabouts at any time when using the car other than for routine transportation to and from school.

MISCELLANEOUS AGREEMENTS

1. We agree that the car is owned by Parent and is for Child's use under the following conditions:
   (a) Unrestricted use shall be attendant upon achieving a 90 percent/ B+ [adjust for child's abilities] grade average for each quarter in all courses not of an advanced placement (AP) nature.
   (b) Restricted use shall be permitted if grade average, calculated quarterly, shall be above _____ in all non-AP courses.
   (c) No use, for one quarter, if grades fall below _____ in non-AP courses.

2. We agree that any additions or improvements to the car shall be made only upon the approval of its owner.

3. We agree that no one shall at any time smoke in the car or have any alcohol or other drugs in the car.

4. We agree to provide transportation to siblings when doing so will save parents having to drive, such as to and from school when Child is also going to school. We agree that Child is not to be the prime source for his or her siblings' transportation needs. We agree to be amenable to general transportation of siblings when possible in a considerate and negotiable fashion.

5. We agree to park in the designated area at home.

_____   _____
CHILD SIGNATURE   PARENT AND OWNER SIGNATURE

ABOUT THE AUTHOR

Dr. John Whitcomb, an emergency physician in Milwaukee, Wisconsin, attributes his attitude toward teen financial responsibility to his childhood in India. With both parents and grandparents working as missionaries, he and his siblings spent months each year in boarding school and away from their family. Learning to manage the monthly stipend they received from the church for school fees, travel, and clothing was a necessity at an early age.

Whitcomb applied the same basic concepts—trust, responsibility and consequences—to teach his own children financial independence. Other parents took notice, and soon they were incorporating Whitcomb's method into their own family lives.

A graduate of Woodstock school in Mussoorie, U.P., India; College of Wooster, Wooster, Ohio; and Yale University Medical School, Whitcomb has been the founder and director of two separate emergency medical groups and currently manages a 42-physician practice at St. Luke's Medical Center, one of Wisconsin's largest hospitals. He was the initiator of the Wisconsin Medical Society's support for graduated driver's licenses for teens and was recently appointed to the Wisconsin JumpStart Coalition, a national network promoting teen financial competence. He entered emergency medicine as "the place where you can make the most dramatic impact."

Whitcomb and his wife Holly, a clergywoman in the United Church of Christ, live in Elm Grove, Wisconsin, with their two children, David and Kate.

To order copies of **CAPITATE Your Kids**, please complete the form below. (Please feel free to duplicate this form.)

I would like to order____copies of **CAPITATE Your Kids** at $16.95 per copy.

Book Total $ _____

Sales Tax (Wisconsin Residents add 5.1%) ($.86/book) $ _____

Shipping and Handling $ _____
($3.20 for first book; $1.60 for each additional book)

Total Amount Enclosed $ _____

Ordered By:

Name: _____

Address:_____

City: _____

State: _____ Zip: _____

Phone Number: __(_____)_____

Ship To: (If different than above)

Name: _____

Address:_____

City: _____

State: _____ Zip: _____

Checks should be made payable to:

CAPITATE Your Kids

P.O. Box 185, Elm Grove, WI 53122

www. capitateyourkids.com

GROUP DISCOUNTS AVAILABLE